CONTENTS

GROUPED

How small groups of friends are
the key to influence on the social web

PAUL ADAMS

VOICES THAT MATTER™

For Jenny. Thank you.

Grouped: How small groups of friends are the key to influence on the social web
Paul Adams

New Riders
1249 Eighth Street
Berkeley, CA 94710
510/524-2178
510/524-2221 (fax)

Find us on the Web at: www.newriders.com
To report errors, please send a note to errata@peachpit.com

New Riders is an imprint of Peachpit, a division of Pearson Education.

Project Editor: Michael J. Nolan
Development Editor: Rose Weisburd
Production Editor: Becky Chapman-Winter
Copyeditor/Proofreader: Jan Seymour
Book Designer: Mimi Heft
Compositor: Danielle Foster
Indexer: James Minkin

ISBN 13: 978-0-321-80411-2
ISBN 10   0-321-80411-2

9 8 7 6 5 4 3 2 1

Printed and bound in the United States of America

INTRODUCTION

Our world is changing

The world around us is changing rapidly. With the invention and rise of the web, we're seeing the largest increase in the amount of information accessible to us since the printing press was invented over 550 years ago. This is truly a revolutionary time, and it will test much of what we have accepted as fact for hundreds of years. There are four massive shifts that are shaping this new world.

The first shift is the rise in accessible information. The accessibility of information is increasing exponentially and is not going to stop within our lifetime. A single query into a search engine produces millions of results. People are adding information to Wikipedia faster than we can read it. Every single day, hundreds of millions of people post billions of distinct pieces of content online. All of this information is digital, and can be analyzed for patterns.

The second shift is a major change in the structure of the web. It's moving away from being built around content, and is being rebuilt around people. This is correlated with a major change in how people spend their time on the web. They're spending less time interacting with content, and more time communicating with other people.

The third shift is that for the first time, we can accurately map and measure social interaction. Many of our theories can now be quantitatively tested. This is incredibly exciting for researchers, but it will also transform how we think about marketing and advertising. Many things that were previously hard to measure, for example, word of mouth marketing, can now be analyzed and understood. We can now start to measure how people *really* influence other people, and it will change how we do business.

The fourth shift is the dramatic increase in our understanding of how we make decisions. In the past decade, we have learned more about the workings of the brain than in all the time before that. Many of our theories about rational thought have turned out to be false, and we have greatly underestimated the power of our nonconscious brain.

If we want to be successful in this new age of exponentially increasing information and a web built around people, we will need to understand social behavior. We will need to understand how people are connected, how they interact, and how they are influenced by different people in their lives. We will also need to understand how people make decisions, and how the different parts of their brain and their biases drive their behavior.

This book is a foundation upon which to build

Each year, many thousands of research studies are carried out on social behavior. This book is not a comprehensive account of all these studies, which would take up thousands of pages, and would never be read by busy professionals. This book is a synthesis of key studies in related fields, summarized into actionable patterns. The goal of this book is to give people a foundational understanding of social behavior, and how it applies to the future of business.

Many of the examples in the book are from Facebook. Because I work there, I have access to many trustworthy case studies and examples that I can share with readers. Many of the Quick Tips apply just as well to activity on other social networks. The academic reader may at times feel that I have oversimplified, overgeneralized, and talked about causality when we may be dealing with correlation. But this simplification is necessary to make research actionable to business. In this case, I believe that perfect is the enemy of good. People who are busy creating products and building companies don't have time to read full research papers, never mind try to synthesize them to find the larger patterns. But to be successful in reorienting their businesses around people, they need an actionable summary of this data—a foundation around which they can build a strategy. If you are that busy professional, this book is your foundation. It's the beginning, not the end.

How to use this book

This book is your introduction to the patterns behind our social behavior. Humans are social creatures, and an understanding of social behavior on the web will soon be required knowledge for almost all businesses. This book is your guide for the exciting new world that we're collectively creating. I've attempted to write a book that will give you, in a matter of hours, all the basic information you need to rethink your business.

The book is made up of independent sections which are designed to be reused. I hope you find that these sections can be taken in isolation if you choose, and used as input to think of new ways in which your business might support social behavior. When you're creating your next product, your next marketing plan, your next advertising strategy, revisit the relevant sections and brainstorm around established patterns of social behavior.

If you want to get into the detail, I've included references to the main research studies I cite. This is not a comprehensive list, but the references included in these papers will lead you to many more related and fascinating research studies. Now let's get started by looking at how, and why, the web is being rebuilt around people.

The web is changing

HOW THE WEB IS CHANGING

Experiences are better when businesses are built around people

Zynga didn't exist five years ago. They are now the biggest games company in the world. Yet in almost every dimension that the games industry traditionally measures, Zynga's games fall short. They have lower resolution graphics, they are less powerful, they are one dimensional. But they have one feature that the other games don't have: They are built around people and their relationships. When you play a Zynga game, you can see your friends who are also playing and collaborate with them. Zynga built their business around people. Their rise should be no surprise—we've been playing games with others for thousands of years.

The games in the Call of Duty franchise are powerful and photorealistic. Since 2003, ActiVision has produced seven independent Call of Duty games. Total sales stand at 60 million copies.

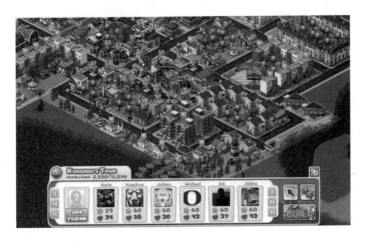

Zynga's CityVille was launched in December 2010. It is less powerful, with much lower-resolution graphics than Call of Duty. It has 110 million users, almost double that of the full Call of Duty franchise, because it is built around people.

When Facebook Photos launched in 2005, there were many other photo products on the market. Facebook Photos was inferior in almost all areas. It supported a lower number of file types, it supported lower resolution photos, and it didn't have many editing features, such as rotating, cropping, or removing red-eye. But Facebook Photos had one feature that the others did not—the ability to tag your friends. Facebook Photos was not built around the content, it was built around the people, and people cared much more about seeing their friends than seeing high-resolution photos, or beautiful landscapes. Facebook Photos quickly became the market leader, supporting more photo uploads than all competitors combined.

Facebook Photos was built around the people in the photos.

Etsy is a commerce website that allows people to sell things that they make. It has a typical commerce website structure, with items for sale broken into categories and sub-categories, and a range of objects featured on the homepage. Etsy is not built around people. Like almost every other commerce website, it's built around content.

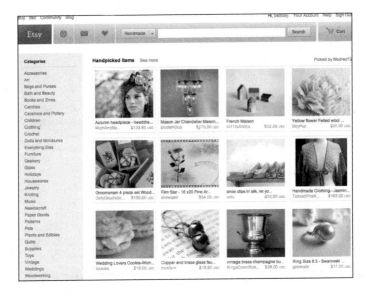

The Etsy homepage has a typical e-commerce layout: categories on the left, editorialized content in the middle. It's not personalized, and it's hard to find a gift for a specific person.

Imagine having to buy a gift for a friend from Etsy. It can be hard to find something you know that friend will like. And the categories that Etsy is structured around don't make it much easier. However, here's where it becomes interesting: Etsy has a version of its website that has been built around people. It connects with Facebook to allow you to choose a friend to buy for, and then reorganizes the content around the things that person has "liked" on Facebook. Suddenly, it's much easier to buy a gift that you think your friend will like.

I can choose which friend to buy for. In this example I'm buying a gift for my brother, Neil.

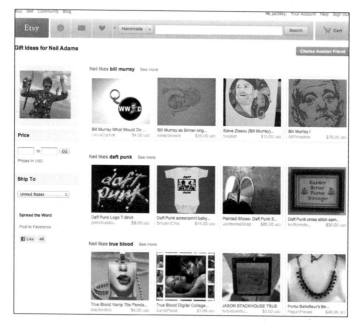

The homepage has changed into things that Neil might like, based on what he has liked on Facebook. Now it's easy for me to buy him a gift.

The web is being rebuilt around people

There is overwhelming evidence that the web is being rebuilt around people. This is not a small change, it's a fundamental re-architecture. We're moving away from a web that connects documents together to a web that connects people together. A person's profile, which tells us the things they care about, and their connections, which tells us who they trust, will move with them as they move from website to website. This fundamental re-architecture of the web is going to affect almost all businesses, because almost all businesses revolve around people. We watch movies and go to concerts with our friends. We ask travel advice and go traveling with our friends. We buy things when we're with friends. We share news with our friends. Even with traditionally conservative business verticals such as finance, we turn to friends for advice—on the best bank to join, or what mortgage rate is reasonable. Businesses that place people, rather than content or technology, at the center of their business model are thriving and in some cases outperforming incumbents.

To be successful on the web, businesses need to understand *why* it's being rebuilt around people as well as understand the behavioral patterns behind this shift.

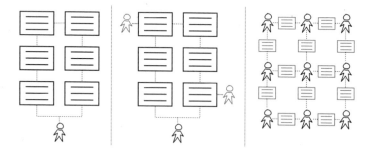

The web is entering its third phase of development. The first phase (left) was documents linked together. For businesses this often meant copying and pasting their print marketing materials online. When we interacted with websites, we couldn't interact with other people. With the second phase (middle) we started seeing opportunities for interaction with others. Some websites had reviews, and ways to leave comments. Many businesses simply added social network buttons to their existing site pages. This was social behavior being bolted on. We are now entering the third phase (right), where websites are being rebuilt around people. Social behavior is the key feature. It is not bolted on.

QUICK TIPS

Don't think about the social web as a set of features to add on to your existing site. The social web is not about adding a "like" button or a "share" button to your web pages. Bolting on social features will not work, because we don't bolt on social behavior offline. We've seen how Zynga, Facebook Photos, and Etsy reinvented businesses by designing around people.

Think of the social web like you think of electricity. It's always there, powering everything else. Social behavior is the same: always there, motivating us to act. It should be placed in the center of the development process.

WHY THE WEB IS CHANGING

Social networks are not new

For thousands of years, people have formed into groups, built strong and weak relationships with others, formed allegiances, and spread rumor and gossip. We have always relied on each other. Humans are social creatures with a need to connect to others; whether we need information, advice, or emotional support, we turn to one another.

Human behavior changes much more slowly than technology

Often, businesses try to understand the social web by focusing on technology and technological change. But they need to focus on human behavior, which changes slowly. Much of our behavior is based on adaptations that took many thousands of years to evolve, and these behavior patterns are not going to change much in our lifetime. Instead, those who are successful with the social web today focus less on the technology itself and more on the communication and interaction it enables with the people they care about. This includes a group size that is hard-wired into our brains by evolution (as you'll see in Chapter 3). Despite huge advances in communication technology over the past 200 years—for example, the invention of the telegraph, telephone, mobile phone, text messaging, instant messaging, and video calling—our social network structure has largely stayed the same. Our modern communications structure allows us to connect to hundreds and sometimes thousands of people, yet we still have a very small number of close friends. Despite the ability of digital communications to connect any two groups of people together, our groups of friends remain independent from each other. Despite being able to call anyone in our mobile phone address book, usually numbering hundreds of people, 80 percent of our phone calls are to the same four people.[1]

We're now seeing the things we have done socially for thousands of years move online. The emergence of the social web is simply our online world catching up with our offline world. Humans first started to live in organized communities with firmly established rules and hierarchy about 10,000 years ago. Going back 2,000 years ago to the Roman Empire, we see a society with very well established laws, governance, and elaborate rules for appropriate social behavior. The web is only about 20 years old; in terms of social behavior, the web is incredibly new. As it matures, the web is aligning itself more closely with how things work offline.

The social web will grow, become mainstream, and eventually be known simply as the web. The businesses that will thrive will be the ones that understand human relationships.

QUICK TIPS

The existing volume of data about people's social behavior can be overwhelming, and it's growing at an increasing pace. Don't get bogged down in the detail. This book will give you the basic and overall patterns you need to understand.

To keep up to date with emerging research, follow the online writings of the people cited throughout this book. Three of the most influential people on how to think about the social web are Duncan Watts, Jonah Lehrer, and Robin Dunbar.

WHY THE SOCIAL WEB IS IMPORTANT TO YOUR BUSINESS

We've seen that the idea of finding overly
influential people was largely a myth

Malcolm Gladwell's 2002 best-selling book *The Tipping Point*
describes The Law of the Few, which states that if you reach
and influence the minority of influential people in society, they
will in turn influence hundreds, thousands, and even millions
of others.[2] Much marketing activity in the last ten years has
been focused on finding and seeding messages with these
"influentials."

This focus on "influentials" is mostly based on a view of
how we *want* the world to work versus how it *actually* works.
Marketing would be easier if these influentials did exist.
However, recent research concludes that it is very rare to see
any one individual influence many other people.[3] Even if the
"influentials" consist of 15 percent of the population, and
generate 30 percent of the conversations about brands (an
optimistic number), people not recognized as "influentials"
still generate 70 percent of the conversations.[4] That 70 percent
of conversations is originating with the people you and I
sit down for dinner with, watch TV with, and work with.
We're now learning that many of our decisions are made
unconsciously (even when we think we made a conscious
decision) and that the people who do have influence over
our behavior are usually the people who are emotionally
closest to us.

We're at the beginning of a cycle in business where we can
move away from this idea of "influentials" and instead focus
marketing activity on small connected groups of close friends.
This shift is what marketers are starting to think about, and
what will be the prominent theme for this decade.

There are three primary driving factors behind this shift, and we have already mentioned the first two. To reiterate, the first driving factor is that our online world is catching up with our offline world. Just as we are surrounded by people throughout our daily life, the web is being rebuilt around people. People are increasingly using the web to seek the information they need from each other, rather than from businesses directly. People always sourced information from each other offline, but up until now, online information retrieval tended to be from a business to a person.

The second driving factor is an acknowledgment in our business models of the fact that people live in networks. For many years, we considered people as isolated, independent actors. Most of our consumer behavior models are structured this way—people acting independently, moving down a decision funnel, making objective choices along the way. Recent research in psychology and neuroscience shows that this isn't how people make decisions. People's networks influence almost every aspect of their lives: what they do, where they go, what brands they prefer, what products they buy. We turn to others to help us make decisions.

The third driving factor in the shift toward small connected groups is that for the first time in humanity, we can accurately map and measure human-to-human interaction. We now have multiple networks that digitally connect hundreds of millions of people, and support communication between these people. We can measure who is connected to whom, who talks to whom, and who shares ideas with whom. This allows us to understand how messages spread and ensure we're reaching the right people with our marketing activity. This understanding will move us away from the dominant form of marketing for the last 50 years: interrupting people to grab their attention. It will move us toward marketing that is based on permission.[5] Toward understanding what people are interested in, making connections with those who are interested, and having those people talk to their friends.

SUMMARY

Experiences are better when businesses are built around people. Many new businesses are using the social web as a platform to change established industries and incumbent companies.

The web is being fundamentally rebuilt around people, and this will change how businesses operate. Almost everything we do revolves around other people, and the social web will reach us all.

This rebuilding of the web is happening because our online life is catching up with our offline life. We're social creatures, and social networks have been around for 10,000 years. The social behavior we've evolved over those thousands of years will be what motivates us to act on the social web. Businesses will need to understand those behavior patterns to be successful.

The social web will change how we think about marketing. What we've already learned from the ability to observe and quantify human relationships has moved us away from the myth of the "influential" and toward understanding how groups of friends talk about businesses, brands, and products.

FURTHER READING

1. Ethnographer Stefana Broadbent has conducted a large amount of research into people's communication behaviors. See her work at usagewatch.org.

2. Malcolm Gladwell's book *The Tipping Point: How Little Things Can Make a Big Difference* (Back Bay Books, 2002) is nicely summarized on Wikipedia, including key ideas and challenges to those ideas.

3. See the 2011 research paper "Everyone's an influencer: Quantifying influence on Twitter" by E. Bakshy and others. The references in this paper point to many similar studies.

4. The marketing consultancy The Keller Fay Group has conducted many studies into how people converse. Explore their data at kellerfay.com/category/insights/.

5. For more information on permission marketing versus interruption marketing, see Seth Godin's book *Permission Marketing: Turning Strangers into Friends and Friends into Customers* (Simon and Schuster, 1999).

2

How and why we communicate with others

WHY WE TALK

We talk to survive

The desire to communicate is hard-wired into all of us. It was
an effective survival mechanism for our ancestors, who shared
information about food supplies, dangerous animals, and
weather patterns, and it continues to help us understand our
world, including what behavior is appropriate and how to act
in certain situations. People talk because sharing information
makes life easier.

Our motivations for sharing online are the same as the
motivations of our ancestors. We often update our status
because we need information. Research has shown that the
majority of tweets that mention brands are seeking information
rather than expressing sentiment, and one in five tweets is
about a product or service.[1]

We talk to form social bonds

Decades of research in social psychology has shown that
people talk to form and grow social bonds. Conversations
ensure that we understand one another. One key aspect of this
is communal laughter. Research has shown that if people laugh
together with strangers, they are as generous to them as they
are to their friends.[2]

Talking to someone sends out strong social signals. It shows
people that we consider them important enough to spend time
together. This is also true online. People update their status
to produce a feeling of connectedness, even when people are
geographically distant.[3] Status updates often contain social
gestures and people often respond by liking or commenting
on the content, not because they actually like the content
but because they want to send out a social signal to build the
relationship. In many cases, the conversation that follows

a status update is much more important than the status update itself. More than the act of *sharing* content, marketing campaigns need to support *conversations*.

Research has shown that social bonds are central to our happiness. The deeper the relationships someone has, the happier they will be.[4] Women talk to form social bonds more often than men. Many of their conversations are aimed at building and maintaining their social network. Men more often talk about themselves or things they claim to be knowledgeable about, often because they are trying to impress the people around them.[5]

We talk to help others

When researchers have studied why people share, they have consistently found that many do it to help others. This is an altruistic act with no expected reciprocity. For many, it is important to them to be perceived as helpful, and so they try to share content that they think other people will find valuable.[6] This is especially clear when we see people share information that may not reflect positively on themselves.

We talk to manage how others perceive us

While people talk to make their lives easier, to form social bonds, and to help others, most of our conversations are a form of reputation management.[7] Research has shown that most conversations are recounting personal experiences, or gossiping about who is doing what with whom. Only 5 percent is criticism or negative gossip. The vast majority of these conversations are positive, as we are driven to preserve a positive reputation.[8]

Our identities are constantly shaped and refined by the conversations we have. Our values were passed on from conversations with our family, community, society, country, church, and through our profession, and are continually refined by the people we spend time with.

WHAT WE TALK ABOUT

Many of our conversations are about other people

One study on what people talk about found that about two thirds of conversations revolve around social issues. Another study found that social relationships and recounting personal experiences account for about 70 percent of conversations. Of the conversations about social relationships, about half are about people not present. The anthropologist Robin Dunbar described these conversations as "Who is doing what with whom, and whether it's a good or bad thing, who is in and who is out, and why."[5] Conversations about other people and their behavior help us understand what is socially acceptable in different situations by revealing how the people we're talking to react to the behavior of the person not present.

Understanding how others have acted, as well as how the people we care about and trust react to those actions, shapes our behavior. It shapes what ideas we agree with, and how we may behave in the future. Supporting conversations about other people is critical for social products and for marketing campaigns based on social behavior.

We share feelings, not facts

Creative agencies the world over try to create content that people will spread. In order to do so, they need to understand what people share, and why. The vast majority of "viral" campaigns don't spread at all, and this is often because the content is factual. Many research studies have shown that people don't share facts, they share feelings.[9]

Jonah Berger and Katherine Milkman studied the most-emailed articles on the *New York Times* over more than a six-month period, totaling 7,500 items. They expected to find content that included factual information that might help others, such as diets or gadgets, but instead found that people shared the content that triggered the most arousing emotions. This included positive emotions such as awe, and negative emotions such as anger and anxiety. Emotions that were not arousing, for example sadness, did not trigger sharing of content.[10]

Content that is positive, informative, surprising, or interesting is shared more often than content that is not, and content that is prominently featured is shared more often than content that is not, but these factors are minor compared to how arousing the content is.

These findings have important implications for advertising. BMW ran a successful campaign called "The Hire," which induced feelings of anxiety through elaborate car chases and generated millions of views. Content that is non-arousing, for example, content that makes people feel comfortable and relaxed, is unlikely to be shared. Public health information may spread more effectively if it induces feelings of anxiety rather than sadness.[11]

We talk about the things that surround us

Our everyday offline conversations tend to be about whatever comes to mind, independent of how interesting it is. And what usually comes to mind first is what is in our current environment (we'll see later how this works for brands). If we're talking to good friends, even our desire to appear interesting takes a backseat to environmental cues. Although we do craft our conversations in order to shape others' perceptions of us,[6] most day-to-day conversations with people we know well are about everyday things and are cued by our environment.

Conversely, our desire to appear a certain way to others is a bigger factor in what we talk about online than offline. Offline, many of our conversations are driven by a need to avoid awkward silences. While people most often talk about what is visible or cued by their environment offline, when online they don't need to fill a conversation space so they can think more carefully about what might be interesting to others.

We talk about brands in passing

The research firm Keller Fay estimates that people talk about approximately 70 brands every week, an average of 10 a day.[12] We might imagine that people talk at length about the pros and cons of competing brands, but most of the time this is not so. Most references to brands in conversations happen in passing. People are talking about something loosely related to the brand, the brand comes up for a few sentences, and then disappears, as the conversation continues about the core topic. When people talk about brands, they are usually not motivated by the brand but by the instinct to converse with others and fill conversation spaces. We need to understand the incidental nature of brand conversations when planning marketing campaigns.

Research has shown that around Halloween, when there are more environmental cues about the color orange, products that are orange (Reese's Pieces, orange soda) are more top of mind.[13] Other research found that products that are cued by the surrounding environment are talked about 22 percent of the time, versus 4 percent for products not cued by the environment. Products that are publicly visible are talked about 19 percent of the time, versus 2 percent for products that are not publicly visible. For example, in one research study, upcoming concerts were talked about much more often when there were CDs in the room.[14] We talk about eating much more often than technology or media, yet many assume that the latter are objectively more interesting.

This has profound implications for understanding how people talk about brands. Products that are visible and accessible will be talked about more. Products that are not naturally in people's environment need to build associations with things that *are* in people's environments. Yet, samples are not a substitute for the actual thing. Coupons and samples do not drive more conversations, but giving people the full product to try, so that it is consistently in the person's environment, can lead to a 20 percent increase in conversations about that product.[14]

Interesting (arousing) products are talked about more initially, but once the novelty wears off, they are talked about less than things cued by people's environments. Frequency of use also drives conversations, as products used frequently are easier to recall from memory and are therefore more top of mind.[15, 16, 17] People talk about big brands far more often than smaller brands. This is not surprising, as bigger brands are more accessible—more visible and easier to recall from memory.

Because we communicate much more frequently with the small number of people we are emotionally closest to, about half of conversations that mention brands are with a partner or family member.[12] Of these brand conversations, 71 percent are face to face, 17 percent are on the phone, and only 9 percent are online.[12] When it comes to spreading ideas, we need to target people's closest ties.

QUICK TIPS

Online posts that ask people to talk about others are likely to have high engagement rates. Many brands ask people to mention others in their responses, like this example from Jameson Irish Whiskey.

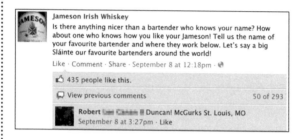

Polls are a great way to drive conversations about your business because the lightweight nature of interaction makes them more aligned with how brands bubble up and dissipate in natural conversations, like this example from Target.

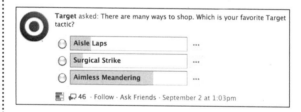

Build campaigns around content that generates strong feelings, as it's more likely to be shared. Marmite is a food brand in the UK that is either loved or hated by people. To generate sharing from the people who hate Marmite, they created a Facebook page called "The Marmite Hate Party."

If you're trying to get people to talk about your brand, put it in their physical environment, as people will talk about things that surround them. Huggies had people upload their favorite photos of their babies to Facebook and then had the most popular photos printed on buses and in subway stations.

WHO WE TALK TO

Most of our communication is with the people closest to us

We like to think that we talk to a wide and diverse set of people, but the reality is that we talk to the same, small group of people again and again. Research shows that people have consistent communication with between 7 and 15 people, but that most conversations are with our five strongest ties. We communicate with the same 5 to 10 people 80 percent of the time.[2] Keller Fay found that 27 percent of our conversations are with our spouse/partner, 25 percent are with a family member, and 10 percent are with a best friend. That's 62 percent of our conversations with the people closest to us. Only 5 percent of our conversations are with acquaintances, and only 2 percent are with strangers. The remaining 31 percent is with the rest of the people in our social network.[12]

Research shows that people use social networks primarily to strengthen the bonds with their strong ties, and secondarily to build relationships with weak ties. When we looked at how many different people members communicated with directly on Facebook every week, including private messages, chats, wall posts, and likes and comments on status updates, we saw that the average was just 4 people. When we looked at how many different people they communicated with every month, it was only 6 people. This is despite the fact that these people are checking Facebook almost every day.[18] Other research has shown that the more people see each other in person or talk on the phone, the more they communicate online.[19]

We can map how frequently we communicate with others onto our social network structure:

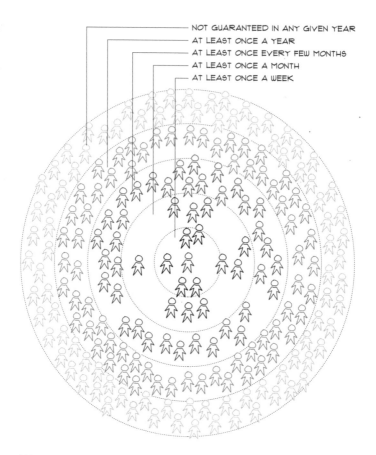

NOT GUARANTEED IN ANY GIVEN YEAR
AT LEAST ONCE A YEAR
AT LEAST ONCE EVERY FEW MONTHS
AT LEAST ONCE A MONTH
AT LEAST ONCE A WEEK

We communicate more with the people toward the center of our
social network, the people we are emotionally closest to.

Who is listening to us changes what we talk about

Who we talk to online has a large impact on what we talk
about. Many people think carefully before posting status
updates. Sometimes they have an explicit audience in mind
for the post and need to consider whether it will be interesting
or offending to the rest of the people they are connected to.

People are very conscious of being seen to be communicating information others will find interesting, funny, or useful. As they usually see only positive feedback, for example "likes" or comments on Facebook posts, it's hard for them to know what other people find valuable. For many people the only way is to look at posts that receive no feedback, assume people didn't find it interesting, and factor the characteristics of that post into future decisions about whether to post something. Sometimes people post updates broadly, as receiving serendipitous replies outweighs any risk of communicating uninteresting information to others.

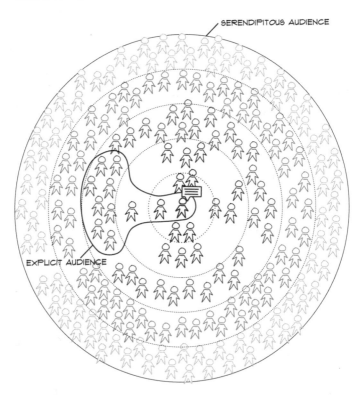

We communicate differently to explicit groups of friends compared with larger groups of people.

When we talk in public, we're very careful about what we say. For example, online public ratings tend to be disproportionately positive when they're linked to our real identity. This is especially true when the other party involved can reciprocate. When people post anonymously, their ratings tend to be almost 20 percent lower than when they use their real names. When ratings are not visible to the party being rated, people give negative reviews more frequently.[20]

> ## QUICK TIPS
>
> We need to build marketing campaigns around the people we're closest to. When BMW launched the new Mini Cooper in the US, they didn't target people in the market for a car or people who fit their customer profile. They instead targeted existing Mini owners, as they knew that these people were the best way to influence their friends.[21]

SUMMARY

People talk for a variety of reasons: Sharing information makes life easier, talking helps to grow social bonds with others, and choosing what we talk about allows us to manage how others perceive us.

We talk about other people, what's around us, and things that generate strong feelings. Most conversations involve recounting personal experiences, or gossiping about who is doing what with whom.

We talk about brands in passing, often driven by what we see in our environment, and to fill a conversation space with someone else.

Most of our communication is with the people closest to us. We communicate with the same 5 to 10 people 80 percent of the time.

FURTHER READING

1. See the 2009 research paper "Twitter power: Tweets as electronic word of mouth" by researchers at Pennsylvania State University and Twitter.

2. See the 2011 research paper "Social laughter is correlated with an elevated pain threshold" by Robin Dunbar and others.

3. See the 2010 research paper "Is it really about me? Message content in social awareness streams" by researchers at Rutgers University.

4. For a great overview of research on happiness, see Derek Bok's book *The Politics of Happiness: What Government Can Learn from the New Research on Well-Being* (Princeton University Press, 2010).

5. See Robin Dunbar's book *How Many Friends Does One Person Need?* (Faber and Faber, 2010).

6. See the 2008 research paper "Word-of-mouth as self-enhancement" by Andrea Wojnicki and David Godes.

7. For two examples, see the 1992 *Social Psychology Newsletter* article "The truth about gossip," and the 1990 article "A social psychology of reputation," both by Nick Emler.

8. See Robin Dunbar's book *Grooming, Gossip, and the Evolution of Language* (Harvard University Press, 1998).

9. See the 2009 research paper "Emotion elicits the social sharing of emotion: Theory and empirical review" by Bernard Rimé.

10. See the forthcoming 2012 research paper "What makes online content viral?" by Berger and Milkman.

11. This example is from the 2011 research paper "Arousal increases social transmission of information" by Jonah Berger.

12. The marketing consultancy Keller Fay have conducted many studies into how people converse. Explore their data at kellerfay.com/category/insights/.

13. See the 2008 research paper "Dogs on the street, Pumas on your feet: How cues in the environment influence product evaluation and choice" by Jonah Berger and Gráinne Fitzsimons.

14. See the 2011 research paper "What do people talk about? Drivers of immediate and ongoing word-of-mouth" by Jonah Berger and Eric Schwartz.

15. See the 1977 social psychology research from Tory Higgins, William Rholes, and Carl Jones.

16. See the 1982 research paper "Memory and attentional factors in consumer choice: Concepts and research methods" by John Lynch and Thomas Srull.

17. See the 1990 research paper "Recall and consumer consideration sets: Influencing choice without altering brand evaluations" by Prakash Nedungadi.

18. Statistics from internal analysis at Facebook.

19. See the 2006 report "The strength of internet ties" by the Pew Research Center.

20. See the 2010 research paper "I rate you. You rate me. Should we do so publicly?" by researchers at the University of Michigan, and the 2007 research paper "A familiar face(book): Profile elements as signals in an online social network" by researchers at Michigan State University.

21. MINI's innovative marketing strategy is described by Charlene Li and Josh Bernoff in their book *Groundswell: Winning in a World Transformed by Social Technologies* (Harvard Business Press, 2008).

3
How we're connected influences us

THE STRUCTURE OF OUR SOCIAL NETWORK

We are born into a network

We are born into relationships: our parents, our family, their friends. Our social network is made up of all the people we're connected to, all the people they are connected to, all the people they are connected to, and so on.

As we grow older, we develop our own relationships, which change throughout our lives. We become closer to some people, we lose touch with others. We can largely control who we are connected to—we can decide who to spend time with, and when to invest in building a relationship. We can also control how interconnected our friends are by deciding whether to introduce them to one another.

We can largely control how central we are in our network. If we maintain more connections, we are more likely to hear the latest gossip, but also more likely to catch the flu.[1] Or we may prefer to be on the periphery, and keep the number of our connections small.

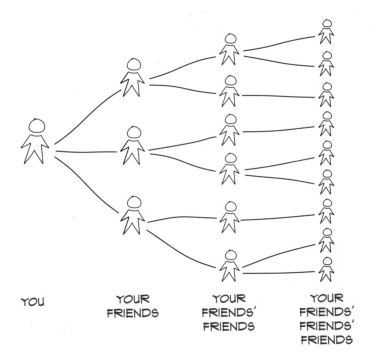

| YOU | YOUR FRIENDS | YOUR FRIENDS' FRIENDS | YOUR FRIENDS' FRIENDS' FRIENDS |

We're connected to people we don't know.

Our social networks evolve

The size and structure of our social networks remain very stable over time, but we do meet new people, and grow close to some of them, while we lose touch with others.

Scientist Albert-László Barabási found that networks were governed by three laws.[2] The first law is *growth*. As people go about their lives, they make new connections and the network grows. We tend to keep the connections we have, and add the new ones. One example of this is on Facebook, where we tend to add more people than we remove, and our friend count tends to slowly increase over time. The second law is *preferential attachment*. People with more connections tend to get even more connections. When all else is equal, our bias is to connect to the people who are already heavily connected. The third law is *fitness*. Fitness describes how desirable it is to connect to that person. Their higher fitness could be from a range of factors including credibility, trust, domain knowledge, and so on. People with higher fitness are deemed more desirable to connect to, and are connected to more frequently.

Managing our evolving networks is one of the challenges of the social web. Offline, this happens organically and subtly. We call less, text less, meet less. We naturally grow apart. Online, things tend to be more black or white, and we tend not to break ties with others for fear of social repercussions. Managing who we are connected to online will be a challenging design problem for many years to come. We're seeing the beginning of solutions such as Facebook Smart Lists, which group your friends based on shared context and on how close you are to them. Google Circles is another attempt to make connection management easier.

Homophily limits who we are connected to

With the rise of the social web, it's tempting to think that we now connect with a very diverse set of people. The fact is that we connect with people like us. This principle, known as homophily, has been comprehensively researched, and it is one of the fundamental patterns of how social networks are structured.

We're separated from others across different dimensions. These dimensions include geography, race, income, education, religion, personal interests, access to technology, and even our genes. When Facebook and MySpace were both popular and frequently used by millions, researcher danah boyd found that Facebook and MySpace were used by very different segments of the population.[3]

The number of our connections follows a common pattern: 5–15–50–150–500

Most people's social networks have a common pattern, and this pattern has remained largely unchanged for thousands of years. There are clear boundaries based on the number of connections we have; it starts at five and goes up by a factor of three.[4]

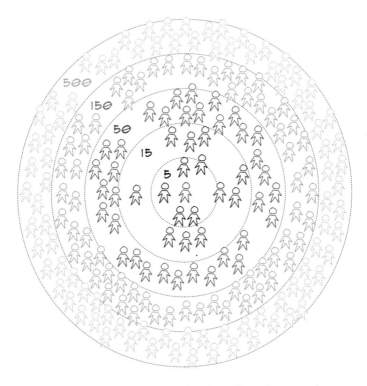

Our social networks tend to have clear boundaries, from people we care a lot about (in the center) to people we loosely know (on the periphery).

Our social network starts with our inner circle, which typically includes up to 5 people. As our core group, we turn to these people for advice, for emotional support, and in times of trouble.

Beyond this is a group of between 12 and 15 people. This group is known to social psychologists as the sympathy group. It's all the people whose deaths would leave you distraught.

Beyond this is a group of about 50 people. These are the people who you communicate with on at least a semi-regular basis. This is the last group where you could confidently say you know about something that happened to them recently, or are generally aware of how they are doing.

Beyond that is a group of about 150. These are the people with whom you can maintain stable social relations. You know each of these people, and you know which of them know each other. Once a group goes beyond this number, we start to observe antisocial behavior, with people no longer acting in the best interests of the group. Evolutionary anthropologist Robin Dunbar has observed that this number repeats itself throughout history. Neolithic villages tended to separate into two once they increased beyond 150 inhabitants, as the behavior of group members could no longer be maintained by peer pressure alone. The Roman army was split into groups of about 150 so that everyone in the group knew each other and would stick together.[4] Group cohesion in online games collapses when the group reaches about 150 active users. Wikipedia involvement tends to plateau at about 150 active administrators.[5] The number of sick days per employee increases dramatically once the business reaches 150 employees.[4] This number, 150, is a physiological limit of our brain. We may have many more connections than 150, but we don't know what is happening in their lives. Regardless of what technology we introduce, this physiological limit will remain the same.

The next group is about 500 people. These are our weak ties—friends of friends, people we meet occasionally, or people we met recently. These are people you know but don't feel close to. We have met many more than 500 people in our lifetime, but beyond 500 we stop recognizing their names. People with more than 500 friends on Facebook often have a hard time figuring out who some of the people are.

It's critical for marketers and designers to understand and internalize this structure. It impacts who communicates with whom, who trusts whom, and how ideas spread.

QUICK TIPS

Marketers currently segregate by demographics and psychographics, but in the future they'll need to segregate by social network structure. Sometimes it will be better to design for, and seed messages with, a small number of specific people. They will need to consider whether they are trying to start conversations among close friends, or among people who loosely know each other but have similar interests. Supporting conversations among friends can drive significant sales. Both Ticketmaster and Eventbrite have made it easy for people to share what events they're attending with their friends on Facebook. For *every link* that was shared, each company saw incremental ticket sales of $5.30 and $2.52, respectively. People saw what their friends were going to and bought tickets too. This is more efficient, and more measurable, than any print or display ad campaign.

Content will tend to stay within boundaries set by network structures. Marketers will need to analyze their target audience across dimensions like geography, race, income, education, religion, personal interests, and access to technology, and account for the fact that high diversity across dimensions may prevent the spreading of information.

PEOPLE NATURALLY FORM GROUPS

We have evolved to form groups

Groups helped our ancestors stay safe from their predators, and helped communities survive through the toughest of conditions. Needing to belong to groups is hard-wired into all of us. Many research studies have shown that

- We have a tendency to form groups, some of which are based on very arbitrary characteristics.
- People will make considerable sacrifices for the benefit of their group.
- In certain situations, groups think better than individuals.[6] It was wise of our ancestors to stick together.

Most people have independent groups of friends that don't overlap

When we study how our social networks are structured, we see that we don't have one cohesive group where all the members know each other. We have different independent groups, and the people in each of these groups do not know the people in the other groups.

Our groups are independent. Our friends from college don't know our friends from when we lived in a different city, and they don't know our family members. Every one of us uniquely connects others together.

The critical point about people having independent groups of friends is that each one of us uniquely connects multiple groups of people together. All of us know unique sets of people. For example, imagine you have a group of friends from where you grew up, and you have a separate group of friends from where you live now. You're probably the only person on this planet who connects those groups of people together. If a message were to pass from one group to the other, it would have to pass through you.

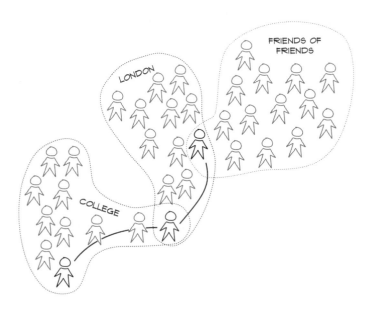

The only way for a message to pass from college friends to London friends, and to their friends, is through you. No other person can pass messages between these groups.

Large populations are made up of these many small connected groups of friends who are often interlinked by unique individuals. When we think about how information spreads, we need to understand that the only way it can pass between these independent groups of friends is through the unique individual who connects them. In other words, the only way information can spread through a large population is through many regular people just like you. This runs counter to the idea that society has very influential people who are necessary for ideas to spread. Social networks of *connected independent groups of friends* is the most important observation in this book, and we'll revisit it multiple times. It is better to design for, and target messages at, many small groups of friends rather than look for overly influential individuals.

We have four to six groups formed around life stage, hobbies, and shared experiences

We've already seen how people have multiple groups of friends. Most people have between four and six groups of friends, and each group usually contains fewer than ten people; the average is four group members. The people in each group know each other well, but they don't know the people in the other groups.[6]

Many of us are surprised to hear that our groups of friends are so small, as we think we interact with many others. But think about the groups of friends in your life. How many do you have? How big are they? Do the people in the different groups know each other? It's very likely that your social network contains a small number of groups, with a small number of group members, and the people in different groups don't know each other.

The groups in our social network form around life stages, shared experiences, and shared interests. For example, all of us have a "Family" group, which we were born into. If we are married we have a second "Family" group, independent from the first one. We have groups of friends from where we grew up, from our school, from our university. In university many of us had groups from our class, groups from our dorms, groups from our activities. If we lived in different places we have groups of friends from each of those locations: our "New York friends," our "London friends," our "San Francisco friends." And we have groups from our interests, our hobbies, the sports we play. Because all of us don't have all these experiences, and we lose touch with many people throughout our lives, the number of our groups tends to stay between four and six.

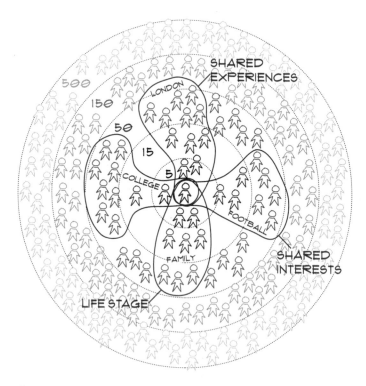

Our groups form around life stages, shared experiences, and shared interests.

QUICK TIPS

Create content that is likely to resonate with small groups of friends, rather than content that is aiming for universal appeal across large populations. Ensure the content is something people are likely to chat about offline. Content that close friends share will spread from group to group to group, and can end up reaching millions of people. But you need to specifically design for the small group of friends for the content to spread.

Forget the idea of "influentials." Go back to basics and focus on everyday people who are interested in the space your business operates in, and the conversations they have with their friends. Simple things can have large returns. American Eagle Outfitters made it easy for people to share what clothes they liked with their Facebook friends. They saw a 57 percent increase in sales.

Focus on getting your message shared within a group as much as you focus on getting it to spread between groups. Messages shared within a group are likely to be relevant to more members of the group, as the members often have similar attitudes and interests. Trying to force content to spread from group to group can lead to that content being perceived as spam.

SOCIAL NETWORK STRUCTURE CHANGES HOW WE'RE INFLUENCED

We are largely in control of who we are connected to, but not in control of who they are connected to

We can control who we are connected to, but we can't control who our connections are connected to, and we can't control who our connections' connections are connected to, even though various influences from these connections can be transmitted to us.

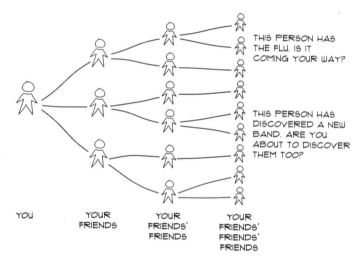

THIS PERSON HAS THE FLU. IS IT COMING YOUR WAY?

THIS PERSON HAS DISCOVERED A NEW BAND. ARE YOU ABOUT TO DISCOVER THEM TOO?

YOU

YOUR FRIENDS

YOUR FRIENDS' FRIENDS

YOUR FRIENDS' FRIENDS' FRIENDS

It's hard for us to see how people we're not directly connected to influence us.

Many research studies show that although we are all connected by less than six degrees, we are only influenced by people up to three degrees away from us. In other words, our friends' friends' friends.[1]

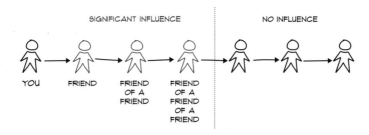

SIGNIFICANT INFLUENCE   NO INFLUENCE

YOU   FRIEND   FRIEND   FRIEND
                   OF A   OF A
                   FRIEND   FRIEND
                               OF A
                               FRIEND

We are only influenced by people up to three degrees away from us.

We are all connected by less than six degrees, but finding the shortest path is hard

You're probably familiar with the theory that everyone on this planet is connected by less than six degrees. This idea is based on an experiment conducted in the 1960s by the social psychologist Stanley Milgram. He had people attempt to send letters to others, knowing only their names, in the shortest number of steps. He reported that on average, a letter passed through 6 people to reach its target.[7] Recent studies analyzing connections online have found similar results. A researcher at Microsoft analyzed 30 billion instant messaging conversations on MSN and concluded that, on average, we are all connected through 6.6 people.[8]

We mistakenly think that six degrees of separation means that it's easy to reach millions of people with our marketing messages. The problem is that six degrees sounds like a short distance when in fact it is very large.

When we speak of five intermediaries, we are talking about an enormous psychological distance between the starting and target points. We should think of the five points as being not five persons apart, but five circles of acquaintances apart—five structures apart. This helps to see it in its proper perspective.

—Stanley Milgram.[9]

Six degrees of connectedness is misleading on two related fronts. First, finding the shortest path between people is very hard. You and I may be two degrees apart, but it's hard for me to find out who we both know.[10] Second, we may be six steps away from any person in the world, but we're therefore also six steps away from *anything* in the world, which makes finding the shortest path incredibly complex.[2]

ME   JOHN   YOU

When you meet someone new, it's hard to find out if you know someone in common, and incredibly hard to find out if your friends know someone in common. In this example, it's hard for me to find out that we both know John.

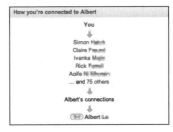

Both Facebook (top) and LinkedIn (bottom) surface common connections. However, there is an enormous difference between being two degrees away from someone (top and bottom left) and being three degrees away from someone (bottom right). Connecting to the person three degrees away involves a lot more work to find the right introduction and it's almost impossible to see beyond your direct connections.

Homophily restricts the spreading of ideas

Because we're only connected to people like us, it's hard for ideas to pass between groups who are separated by dimensions like race, income, and education.[9] When people are separated in multiple dimensions, they perceive each other as far apart even though they may be connected, and if people perceive each other as far apart, they're unlikely to share things.

Homophily indicates that people are unlikely to be influenced by celebrities whose lifestyles are very different from our own. If our behavior were influenced by celebrities, our bodies would all be as slim as theirs. The personal care brand Dove took advantage of this observation with its Campaign for Real Beauty.[11] The women in the campaign were perceived as "people like me," and had greater influence than celebrities or beauty experts.

QUICK TIPS

When we're planning marketing campaigns, we should concentrate on content that is likely to spread among friends, and friends of friends, but we shouldn't expect it to spread to people more than three degrees away from the people who first encountered the message. This is why it's important to seed the content with *many* small groups.

Using existing connections is a powerful way to build new connections. It highlights the shortest paths between people, which can be useful for sharing information to more relevant groups, or connecting with new people. Airbnb is a service that allows people to rent out their homes to strangers. As these people don't know each other, which makes it hard to know who to trust, Airbnb used Facebook connections to make it possible to see whether you are connected to the other people through friends of friends. It's now easy to ask the mutual friend about whether we're likely to get on well with the host, or whether we're likely to like their place.

Introducing **Airbnb Social Connections**

With Airbnb Social Connections, you can now find places to rent in your personal network.

See your connections

SUMMARY

Our social network is made up of all the people we're connected to (which we can largely control) and all the people they're connected to (which we can't control). Your friends' friends' friends, usually people you don't know, can have a dramatic impact on your behavior and the decisions you make.

Most people's social networks have a common pattern:

· The 5 people in your inner circle

· Up to 15 people you are very close to

· About 50 people you communicate with semi-regularly so that you generally know what is going on in their lives

· About 150 people with whom you can maintain stable social relations

· About 500 weak ties, people you loosely know and can recognize

Most people have independent groups of friends that don't overlap. This means that every one of us uniquely connects multiple groups of people together, so if messages are to spread, they have to pass through the people who connect groups. In other words, the people who spread ideas are just regular people. Everyone is uniquely connected to others, so to spread across populations, we need to persuade regular people to pass the message on. In this sense, everyone is an influencer. Although some people have more influence than others, it is very rare to see any one individual influence many other people. The structure of our social networks is much more important in spreading ideas than the characteristics of individual people.

Most people have between four and six groups of friends, and each group usually contains fewer than 10 people. It's tempting to think that we're connected to a very diverse set of people but we're connected to people like us. This restricts the spreading of ideas, as it's hard for ideas to pass between groups that are separated by dimensions like race, income, and education.

FURTHER READING

1. In their book *Connected: The Surprising Power of Our Social Networks and How They Shape Our Lives* (Little, Brown, 2009), Nicholas Christakis and James Fowler draw on a large body of research to illustrate how we are influenced by our friends' friends' friends. Examples they use include giving up smoking and losing weight.

2. See Albert-László Barabási's book *Linked: How Everything Is Connected to Everything Else and What It Means* (Plume, 2003).

3. See the research paper "White flight in networked publics? How race and class shaped American teen engagement with MySpace and Facebook," first published in 2009 by danah boyd.

4. For an in depth discussion on the structure of our social network and how it's shaped by evolution, see the 2010 book *How Many Friends Does One Person Need?* by Robin Dunbar. Nicholas Christakis and James Fowler have also studied this in modern groups. See the 2010 *Harvard Magazine* article "Networks, neolithic to now" for an overview.

5. For a great overview (with data) of Dunbar's number and online games, see Christopher Allen's post "The Dunbar number as a limit to group sizes" on his blog *Life With Alacrity*.

6. For lots of detail about group dynamics, see David Brook's book *The Social Animal: The Hidden Sources of Love, Character, and Achievement* (Random House, 2011).

7. For more information on Stanley Milgram's experiments, including challenges to his methods, see the Wikipedia article on *Small world experiment*.

8. See the 2008 research paper "Planetary-scale views on a large instant-messaging network" by Jure Leskovec and Eric Horvitz (where they analyzed 30 billion conversations among 240 million MSN users).

9. Quote from Stanley Milgram's 1967 *Psychology Today* article "The small-world problem."

10. In his book *Six Degrees: The Science of a Connected Age* (Norton, 2003), Duncan Watts describes the difficulties in finding the shortest paths between people.

11. See the Wikipedia article titled *Dove Campaign for Real Beauty*.

4

How our relationships influence us

RELATIONSHIP TYPES
AND PATTERNS

We have unique relationships with everyone we know

Each relationship between two people is unique. We have
histories with some people that include thousands of distinct
interactions that have shaped how we feel about one another.
We are closer to some people than others, including within
our groups of friends. We trust some of our friends on certain
topics, and trust others on different topics. We turn to some
close friends in times of trouble, but don't feel comfortable
turning to all of them equally. Each of these unique
relationships heavily influence our behavior with others.

We have different types of relationships

Although each relationship is unique, we can categorize some
of their characteristics to help us understand them better.
In their research, Liz Spencer and Ray Pahl identified eight
different types of relationships[1]:

· *Associates* are people who don't know each other well, and
  only share a common activity, such as a hobby or a sport.

· *Useful contacts* are people who share information and advice.
  Typically this is related to our work or career.

· *Fun friends* are people who socialize together primarily for
  fun. They don't have a deep relationship, and don't provide
  each other with emotional support.

- *Favor friends* are people who help each other out in a functional manner but not in an emotional manner.
- *Helpmates* display characteristics of both favor friends and fun friends. They socialize together for fun and also help each other out in a functional manner.
- *Comforters* are similar to helpmates but with a deeper level of emotional support.
- *Confidants* disclose personal information to each other, enjoy each other's company, but aren't always in a position to offer practical help.
- *Soulmates* display all of these elements and are the people we're closest to.

We have a very small number of confidants and soulmates, often numbering fewer than five.

One of the most useful ways to understand our unique relationships is to look at them as strong ties and weak ties. This distinction has been extensively studied by social psychologists and anthropologists. Strong ties are the people you're closest to—your closest friends and family. Weak ties are people you don't know well. Often they include people you have met recently and have yet to form a strong relationship with, and people you know through others, such as friends of friends. Strong ties include our soulmates, confidants, and comforters. Weak ties include our helpmates, favor friends, fun friends, useful contacts, and associates. We'll explore both strong ties and weak ties later in this chapter.

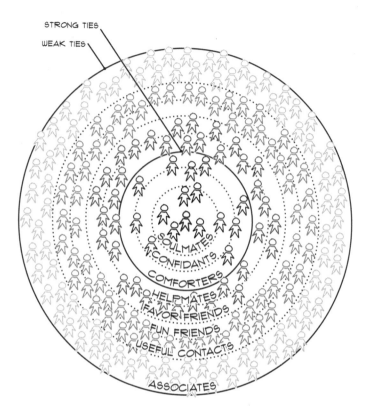

We have a much smaller number of strong ties than weak ties.

We have different patterns of relationships

Researchers have observed different patterns of relationships. We've already seen one relationship pattern focused on the *structure* of the network, how our social network is broken up into independent groups numbering fewer than ten people. When studying the relationship patterns *within* the network, Spencer and Pahl found that people don't have friends from all eight friendship types. In fact, people tend to have friends from distinct groups of relationship types, and they identified four main patterns: Basic, Intense, Focal, and Broad.

Basic friendship patterns include people who only have simple friendships, usually fun friends and associates. They are not close to their family and often deal with emotional issues on their own.

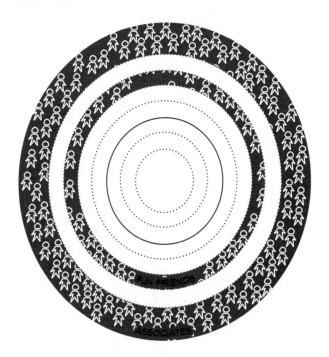

The basic friendship pattern.

Intense friendship patterns include people who only have complex friendships, usually confidants and soulmates. They make a clear distinction between "true friends" and other relationships such as acquaintances.

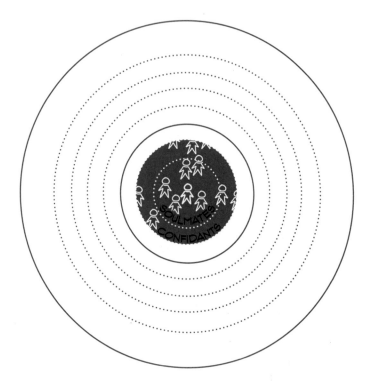

The intense friendship pattern.

Focal friendship patterns include people who have both simple and complex friendships. They usually have a small core of soulmates and confidants, and a much larger group of fun friends.

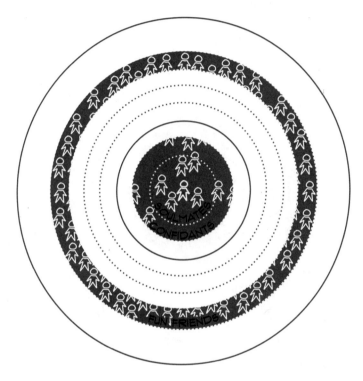

The focal friendship pattern.

Broad friendship patterns include people who have both simple and complex friendships, and who also include a wider range of friendship types. In this kind of pattern, fun friends may be outnumbered by helpmates or confidants, though soulmates rarely number more than one or two.

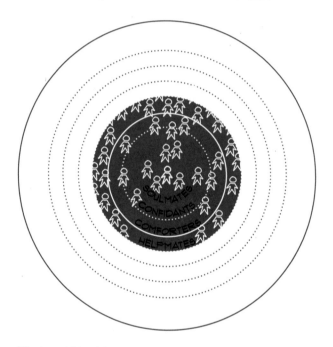

The broad friendship pattern.

STRONG TIES

Strong ties are the people we care about most

Strong ties are our closest friends and family. They are
the people we trust the most, and the people we turn to
for emotional support. Strong ties are very important for
maintaining our wellbeing. Research has shown that people
with strong ties have lower incidents of heart disease, and
get fewer cases of colds and the flu.[2] Family members are
disproportionately represented among our strong ties. Our
strong ties include friends, family, coworkers, and neighbors,
and family can sometimes represent up to half of our strong
ties, despite there being many fewer family members than non-
family members in our social network. When all else is equal,
family gets preference.

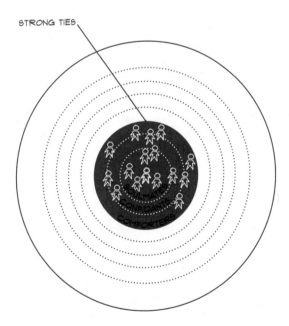

Strong ties are often described as the people in our "inner circle."

We only have a small number of strong ties

Most people have fewer than ten strong ties, and many have fewer than five. We keep our circles of trust very small. One study of 3,000 Americans found that they had between two and six strong ties.[3] A study conducted in 2002 and 2007 found that people had about ten friends and family they meet or speak with at least weekly.[4] Another study of 5,124 adults found that the average number of strong ties was eleven.[4]

Most of our communication is with strong ties

Studies into communication have found that the majority of communication is with the people who are emotionally closest to us, the people most likely to reciprocate our attention.[5] On average, we have ongoing communication with between seven and fifteen people, but 80 percent of that is with the same five to ten people.[6] Eighty percent of our phone calls are to the same four people.[7] Aside from face to face interaction, people communicate with their strong ties primarily through voice calls and text messages, as they view those as being the most reliable communication channels. However, as more people use social networks, and more people have always-on access to social networks on their phones, communication with strong ties on social networks is increasing. Research on social networks has shown that they are primarily being used to strengthen existing relationships rather than build new relationships. In fact, the more people see each other in person and communicate on the phone, the more they communicate online.[8]

On average, people have 160 friends on Facebook yet communicate directly with only four to six of them.[9] We consume updates from many more than that, but when it comes to wall posts, private messages, instant messages, likes, and comments on others' posts, we only communicate with an average of four people per week and six people per month.[9] This is despite the fact that we're checking Facebook almost every day. Another research study tried to understand how many people we spend time with offline by analyzing the tags in Facebook photos. It found that the average person was tagged with six to seven other people.[10] All this data on social network interaction closely reflects our offline life, where many of us have fewer than five strong ties. We're communicating with the same small number of strong ties online as well as offline.[11]

Our strong ties have disproportionate influence over us

Research on decision making has consistently found that we are disproportionately influenced by the people we're closest to emotionally. The strongest influence is between mutual best friends.[12] We're three to five times more likely to share similar preferences with our friends than with strangers.[13] This is not new. Research on voting in the 1940s showed that people were much more heavily influenced by who their family and close friends were voting for than they were by the media.[14] These patterns have held despite the vast changes in technology in the last 70 years. In independent studies, Forrester, Polara, and Edelman all found that people were three to four times more likely to trust a friend or acquaintance than a blogger or expert for product purchase advice.[15, 16, 17] Research on social networks has shown that people only influence, and are influenced by, a small number of other people.[18] Other research has shown that we are influenced by the people that surround us, which often tends to be our strongest ties.[19]

New tools will emerge around strong ties that will change how we buy things

We trust our strong ties, and are more likely to let them know intimate details of our life. This can include what we do, where we go, what we buy, and what we decide not to buy. Assuming they give us permission, in the future we'll be able to see which of our friends have visited certain locations, stores, or websites, and what products or services they bought. We'll be able to see how they rated the experience, and if they haven't explicitly given a rating, we'll be able to directly reach out to them and solicit advice about our potential purchases. All products and services will be filtered through the previous experiences of our friends.

QUICK TIPS

Make it easy for people to get feedback from strong ties on potential purchases by supporting the established communication channels they use: voice calls, text, email, Facebook.

Build campaigns around strong ties, as these are the people who have the most influence over us. For example, seeing more information about a small number of close friends is likely to be more important to people than less information about more people they don't know as well.

WEAK TIES

Weak ties are people we don't know very well

Weak ties are often friends of friends, or people we met recently. We would describe many of our weak ties as acquaintances. We communicate with most of our weak ties infrequently, often going months or even years without direct interaction. We know who our weak ties are, we know them by name and can recognize them, but we don't know much about many of them. We have hundreds of weak ties, but as we saw earlier, we can only keep up to date with about 150 of them.

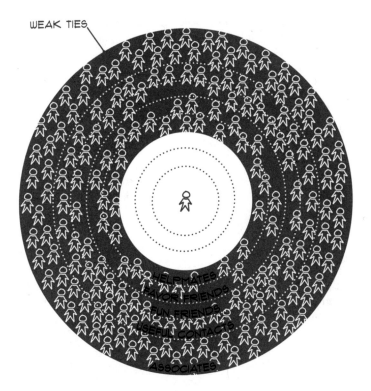

WEAK TIES

HELPMATES
FAVOR FRIENDS
FUN FRIENDS
USEFUL CONTACTS
ASSOCIATES

Weak ties are people we don't know so well.

Online social networks are making it easier to feel connected to many of our weak ties. Although we may not interact directly, we can more easily follow what is happening in their lives than we could before these tools existed, when we relied on gossip to stay up to date. This also introduces some awkward social exchanges that don't exist offline. People are often worried about whether to accept a friend request, or delete a contact, in case they meet that person again. The binary nature of our online tools misses all the subtlety and nuance of our offline interactions with weak ties.

We usually interact with weak ties because of a common interest or object. This could mean meeting up via a mutual friend. Or it could mean interacting because we need to complete a shared task. Other times it might be because we share a hobby or are on the same sports team, or because we're seeking information.

Weak ties can be powerful sources of information

In his seminal research paper on strong and weak ties, sociologist Mark Granovetter found that weak ties are often a better source of information than strong ties.[20] Our weak ties are at the periphery of our social network, which means they are connected to more diverse sets of people than our strong ties, which are more central in our network. These diverse ties pass on more novel information, and so they can often know more than our strong ties do. Our unconscious brain detects this pattern, and instructs us to start searching for information two or three degrees away from us to ensure that we are receiving new information. This pattern has been observed with many things, including finding a new job or finding a good piano teacher.[21]

One downside to sourcing information from our weak ties is that we know less about their knowledge and whether we can trust their judgment. Their credibility is not as well defined as our strong ties. Because of this, surfacing information about our weak ties will be crucial for encouraging interactions between people. We will need to know that our weak ties are qualified to talk about specific topics, and that they are trustworthy.

What this translates to is that encouraging interactions between weak ties is good for business. Research has shown that increases in positive online comments appear a month or two before an increase in market share.[22]

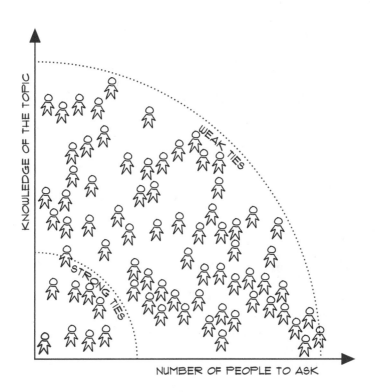

When people are looking for information and opinions from others, they look to their strong ties first because they know they can trust them, even though there are weak ties that have higher knowledge on the topic.

QUICK TIPS

When creating content, consider that although people's weak ties may be more knowledgeable than their strong ties, they may trust them less. It is important to maximize the amount of trust between people. Some ways of doing this include showing their other shared ties, emphasizing their common interests, or exposing their sources of knowledge.

HOW RELATIONSHIPS CHANGE

Our strong and weak ties change slowly over time, often over the course of many years. We meet new people throughout our lives and become closer to some more than others. As we have limited capacity for maintaining stable social relationships, we drift away from other people who we were close to in the past. Some of our weak ties become strong ties as some of our strong ties become weak ties. Sociologist Peter Marsden found that the number of our strong ties decreases gradually as we get older, and this varies depending on whether people went to university or tended to move around and live in different places. People with higher education tended to have double the number of strong ties as those who didn't finish high school.[23]

In their research on friendship, Spencer and Pahl found that some people have bounded relationships where friends are made at a particular life stage and new people remain acquaintances, while others have serial relationships where friends are replaced at each life stage. Others have evolving patterns, where new friends are added at each life stage, but some remain from previous life stages.[1]

QUICK TIPS

We need to keep lists of people, whether that's in a social web application, or a customer marketing database, up to date. We need to know whether people still turn to the same people they did in the past, and whether their trusted sources have changed.

SUMMARY

We have unique relationships with everyone we know and these relationships heavily influence how we behave around others.

One of the most useful ways to think about our unique relationships is to look at them in terms of strong ties and weak ties. Strong ties are the people you're closest to. Weak ties are people you don't know very well.

Many research studies have found that most people have fewer than ten strong ties, and many have fewer than five. We keep our circles of trust very small. The majority of communication is with our strong ties. With a majority of our attention focused on strong tie relationships, it's no surprise that we are disproportionately influenced by the people we're closest to emotionally.

Our weak ties are our acquaintances, and we communicate with them infrequently. Weak ties are often a better source of information than strong ties because they are connected to more diverse sets of people than our strong ties, and these diverse ties pass on more novel information. Hence they can often know more than our strong ties do.

FURTHER READING

1. See the book *Rethinking Friendships: Hidden Solidarities Today* (Princeton, 2006) by Liz Spencer and Ray Pahl.

2. In his book *Viral Loop: From Facebook to Twitter, How Today's Smartest Businesses Grow Themselves* (Hyperion, 2009), Adam Penenberg reviews research studies, including a decade-long Australian study, that indicate how strong friendships are related to better health.

3. In their book *Connected* (Little, Brown, 2009), Nicholas Christakis and James Fowler describe one study they conducted with 3,000 Americans.

4. See research conducted at the Center for the Digital Future at the University of Southern California (digitalcenter.org) in 2002 and 2007.

5. See the 2009 research paper "Social networks that matter: Twitter under the microscope" by researchers at HP Labs.

6. See the article "The small size of our communication network" by Stefana Broadbent on usagewatch.org.

7. This data is from ethnographer Stefana Broadbent's presentation at the TED conference 2009, viewable on YouTube. Broadbent has done much research into how people communicate with each other. You can follow her work at usagewatch.org.

8. See the 2006 report "The strength of internet ties" by the Pew Research Center.

9. Data from internal analysis at Facebook.

10. See the study on Facebook photo tags described in *Connected* (see Item 3 above).

11. Various research shows that almost all friends on Facebook are people who users first met offline. For an overview, see the 2009 research paper "The problem of conflicting social spheres" by researchers at Manchester Business School.

12. In their book *Connected* (see Item 3 above), Nicholas Christakis and James Fowler describe how mutual best friends are most influential, how three degrees of influence works, and the concept of hyperdyadic spread.

13. See research referenced by Andy Sernovitz in *Word of Mouth Marketing* (Kaplan, 2009).

14. See Paul Lazarsfeld's research from the 1940s and 1950s, in particular the books *The People's Choice* (Columbia University, 1944) and *Voting: A Study of Opinion Formation in a Presidential Campaign* (University of Chicago Press, 1954).

15. See Jeremiah Owyang's 2008 post "Who do people trust? (It ain't bloggers)" on his blog at web-strategist.com.

16. The Edelman Trust Barometer 2008 study.

17. Pollara.ca doesn't give access to the study but you can read more about it in the Read Write Web article "Study: There is no tipping point, blog readers are skeptical."

18. See the 2009 research paper "Effects of word-of-mouth versus traditional marketing: Findings from an internet social networking site," by Michael Trusov, Randolph Bucklin, and Koen Pauwels.

19. See Peter Marsden's article "Core discussion networks of Americans" in *American Sociological Review*, 1987.

20. See Mark Granovetter's 1973 full research paper "The strength of weak ties."

21. Granovetter (see Item 20) studied how people look for new jobs, and Christakis and Fowler (see Item 12) studied how people found a new piano teacher.

22. See research described by Charlene Li and Josh Bernoff in their book *Groundswell* (Harvard Business Press, 2008).

23. See Peter Marsden's 1987 full research paper "Core discussion networks of Americans."

5

The myth of the "influentials"

HIGHLY CONNECTED DOES NOT MEAN HIGHLY INFLUENTIAL

Influence is hard to measure

Over the last ten years, marketers have often focused on finding people who disproportionately impact how information is spread, often called "influentials." Much of this thinking was driven by Malcolm Gladwell's best-selling book, *The Tipping Point*, where he describes The Law of the Few. This law states that there are a small number of very influential people in society, and if you reach and influence them, they will influence hundreds, thousands, and even millions of others. Gladwell characterizes "influentials" as highly connected, highly persuasive, and viewed as credible in their field.[1]

As we saw earlier, this focus on "influentials" is mostly based on a view of how we want the world to work versus how it actually works. The network in which word of mouth spreads, including all the people, interactions, and communication channels, is generally unobservable because it is so complex. In addition, when we do try to understand it, we only look at messages that did spread, and can't observe the ones that did not. This complexity has led us to confuse coincidence and correlation with causality.[2,3] We look back after an event has occurred, see the most visible person, and assume they wielded the greatest influence.[4] This is the problem with Gladwell's Law of the Few. It's easier to attribute success to an inspirational person, rather than try to understand the complex network in which they are situated.

People with many connections are not necessarily more influential

Most studies have found little correlation between highly connected people and large degrees of influence. Even when there are influential people and specific situations where they can wield great influence over many others, finding them is so expensive that it becomes a poor investment compared to other available strategies.

Studies on Twitter have shown that mass spreading of ideas is incredibly rare. In one study, 74 million tweets were analyzed. Only a few dozen generated a thousand retweets, and only a couple reached ten thousand retweets. In fact, 98 percent of attempted cascades do not spread at all.[5] Also, Twitter users with the most followers do not necessarily have the greatest number of retweets or the greatest number of mentions.[6]

The structure of our social networks is much more important in spreading ideas than the characteristics of individual people. When Duncan Watts repeated Stanley Milgram's six degrees study but with much larger numbers (60,000 people in 166 countries), he found no "influentials" in the delivery process. People did not pass on messages to people they thought were highly connected, they passed them on to someone who they thought had something in common with the target or to people who they thought would continue to pass the message on.[5]

Trying to find highly influential people is a risky strategy

Although some people *are* more influential than others, they are much rarer than we think, and finding them is an extremely hard and expensive task. The loudest, most visible people are not correlated with influence. Although people who have a high number of connections are more likely than the average individual to set off a cascade of an idea, their success fluctuates wildly, and it is therefore a risky and unreliable strategy to try to find them.[5, 7]

We've also seen that everyone is uniquely connected to others, so to spread across populations, we need to persuade regular people to pass the message on. In this sense, everyone is an influencer. We all influence the people around us to varying degrees. All of us are looked upon by others as knowledgeable about certain topics.

QUICK TIPS

Instead of looking for overly influential people, businesses should look for regular people who are likely to be interested in what they have to say. Targeting large numbers of these people, potentially in the thousands, is more likely to spread ideas than trying to find a small number of influential individuals. These people won't be visible on an individual level. You won't necessarily know them by name. But you will know that they have the right attributes to be interested in what you have to say. Using many of these people to set off many small cascades averages out the random factor, and is more likely to produce consistent positive results.

IDEAS OFTEN SPREAD BECAUSE PEOPLE ARE INFLUENCEABLE

Ideas spread when people have low adoption thresholds

When ideas spread, there are always two parties involved: the person passing on the idea, and the person receiving the new information. We often overlook the person who is receiving the idea and whether they are easy to influence. Researchers call this a person's "adoption threshold." People have varying thresholds for adopting new ideas, and this can differ greatly even on an individual level. For example, someone may be very easy to influence on one topic, but very hard to influence on another topic.

Our threshold is influenced by our past experiences; for example, good or bad experiences with a brand. It is also influenced by whether we have a risk-averse personality or deepset habits.[8] Our threshold can be lowered if we see many people we deem as credible adopting something, for example our friends, family, or people in our community. We often look at how an idea spread and then assign responsibility on the most visible, highly connected people, assuming they had great influence, when in fact the reason the idea spread was because lots of people had low adoption thresholds.

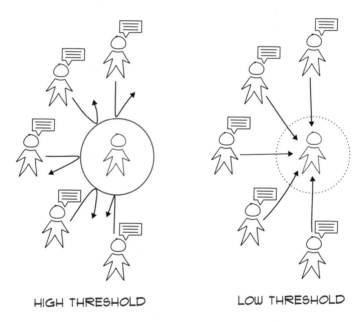

HIGH THRESHOLD   LOW THRESHOLD

It's much easier to influence people with low thresholds to the new idea.

For ideas to spread widely, you need connected groups of easily influenced people

In multiple research studies, Duncan Watts found that the most important factor in determining whether an idea spread was not whether there were influential people, but whether there was a critical mass of easily influenced people who were connected to other people who were easy to influence.[5] When this critical mass of connected people didn't exist, not even the most influential people could get an idea to spread widely. This means that understanding the structure of the network in which you seed ideas is much more important than understanding whether individuals have a high degree of influence.

QUICK TIPS

When creating content, it's important to consider how it will be received by people with high thresholds and low thresholds. Not everyone will see the content in the same way. It may be best to optimize for people with either high or low thresholds, and not try to persuade both.

Consider how to lower people's thresholds. One easy way to do it is to have your product or brand introduced through a person's friend. This is the motivation behind Facebook's Sponsored Stories. Also, try to reinforce your message by having multiple people within the same group repeat it.

HOW HUBS SPREAD IDEAS

There are two types of hubs

When people talk about "influentials," they are usually talking about hubs. Hubs are people with a large number of connections. Typically, we think about hubs as a one-way information channel. They consume information from an official source, and pass it on to all their connections. But in fact, hubs are two-way channels. They have many incoming links as well as outgoing links.[6, 9, 10]

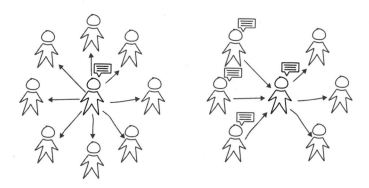

How we typically think about hubs (left) and how we need to think about hubs (right).

There are two types of hubs, and research has shown that both are necessary for mass adoption of a new idea (including new products and brands). Innovative hubs are people who are highly connected and have a low threshold for new ideas. They embrace new ideas after being exposed to them a small number of times. Follower hubs are more common, and are people who are highly connected but have a high threshold for new ideas. Follower hubs tend not to embrace a new idea until they have been exposed to it many times. Innovative hubs initiate the process of spreading a new idea, but follower hubs are more important for ensuring the idea is adopted by the masses. Innovative hubs drive the speed of adoption; follower hubs drive the overall market size. Many marketers only focus their efforts on innovative hubs.

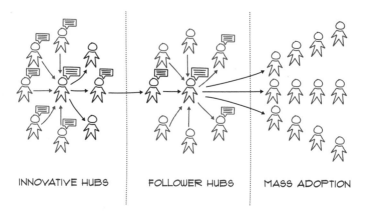

INNOVATIVE HUBS   FOLLOWER HUBS   MASS ADOPTION

Ideas need to start from innovative hubs but need to pass through follower hubs (who often adopt much later) before mass adoption.

We confuse early adoption with influence

The people who adopt products earlier are not necessarily more influential than the people who adopt later. Follower hubs are often late adopters, and the only reason they adopt is because they were continually exposed to so many of their connections adopting. Multiple research studies have shown that a high quality product will ultimately be adopted by people without the recommendation of hubs. Hubs accelerate the process of adoption but are not responsible for it.[11]

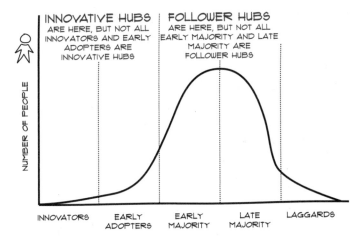

In his seminal book *Crossing the Chasm*,[12] Geoffrey Moore described how products need to cross the chasm from early adopters to early majority in order to succeed in a mass market. Follower hubs are therefore necessary to be successful.

For some industries, acceleration of adoption is critical, and therefore hubs become important. For example, movies generally need to have large opening weekend box office sales to be profitable.

Influence doesn't flow from mass media to the masses

We think about information as a one-way flow from mass media to hubs, and from hubs to large populations. This is how we want the world to work because it makes our jobs easier. It's easy for us to carefully craft our story and send it out into the world via mass media, assuming that it will spread. But social networks do not follow this linear structure. We have seen how hubs are two-way channels, and how our social network structure is made up of many small, interconnected groups.

Because everyone is paying attention to everyone else in social networks, it's incredibly hard for any one person to have great influence. It can happen, but it's usually because they're operating in *small* networks where they do have great influence over the other people, and their small networks are joined to many other small networks who also have a person of great influence.[8]

We've seen that highly connected people do not often set off cascades of ideas, and that overall, cascades are quite rare. When they do occur, they're usually set off by a regular person and not someone who has the characteristics of an "influential." When they are set off by an "influential" they spread further, but it's very rare for this to happen.

QUICK TIPS

Identify and target innovative and follower hubs, as both are necessary for mass adoption. Design different strategies for both types of hubs, and ensure you are measuring both incoming and outgoing connections.

Measure whether someone is a hub. In a study on Cyworld,[13] a large social network in South Korea, researchers proposed a hub to be a person with both in- and out-degrees that are more than three standard deviations above the mean for people within the network.

Consider how to identify influential people. You can start with what interests they have and what brands they buy, as this will give you an idea of whether they have a high or low threshold for your product or brand. Next, consider how many affiliations they have, as people with more affiliations are more likely to be the unique individuals connecting diverse groups. Finally, consider how many connections they have and what brands their connections prefer. Most social networks now allow you to target advertising based on people's interests and preferred brands.

SUMMARY

We usually think that information flows from mass media to hubs, and from hubs to large populations. But social networks do not follow a linear structure. Hubs have many incoming links as well as outgoing links. Innovative hubs initiate the process of spreading a new idea, but follower hubs are more important for ensuring the idea is adopted by the masses. Our social network structure is made up of many small interconnected groups. When cascades of an idea do occur, they are usually set off by a regular person, and not someone who has the characteristics of an influential. When they are set off by an "influential" they spread further, but it's very rare for this to happen.

People have varying thresholds for adopting new ideas, and this can differ greatly on an individual level. The most important factor in determining whether an idea spread was not whether there were influential people, but whether there was a critical mass of easily influenced people who were connected to other people who were easy to influence. When this critical mass of connected people didn't exist, not even the most influential people could get an idea to spread widely. This means that understanding the structure of the network in which you seed ideas is much more important than understanding whether specific individuals have a high degree of influence.

FURTHER READING

1. Malcolm Gladwell's *The Tipping Point: How Little Things Can Make a Big Difference* is nicely summarized on Wikipedia, including key ideas and challenges to those ideas.

2. See the 2009 paper "Distinguishing influence-based contagion from homophily-driven diffusion in dynamic networks" by Sinan Aral, Lev Muchnik, and Arun Sundararajan.

3. See the 1993 research paper "Identification of endogenous social effects: The reflection problem" by Charles Manski.

4. See the work of sociologist Rakesh Khurana. Start with his book *Searching for a Corporate Savior: The Irrational Quest for Charismatic CEOs* (Princeton University Press, 2002).

5. See the 2011 research paper "Everyone's an influencer: Quantifying influence on Twitter" by researchers at Yahoo! Research and the University of Michigan.

6. See the 2010 research paper "Measuring user influence in Twitter: The million follower fallacy" by researchers in Germany, the UK, and Brazil.

7. For a detailed look at how ideas cascade, see Duncan Watts' book *Everything is Obvious: Once You Know the Answer* (Crown Business, 2011).

8. In his book *Six Degrees* (Norton, 2003), Duncan Watts explores high and low thresholds for idea adoption.

9. See the 2010 research paper "What is Twitter, a social network or a news media?" by researchers at KAIST, Korea.

10. See the 2010 research paper "TwitterRank: Finding topic-sensitive influential twitterers" by researchers at Singapore Management University and Penn State.

11. See the research work on word-of-mouth marketing by Barak Libai from Tel Aviv University. Start with his 2001 research paper "Talk of the network: A complex systems look at the underlying process of word-of-mouth."

12. Geoffrey Moore's book *Crossing the Chasm: Marketing and Selling High-Tech Products to Mainstream Customers* (Harper, 1991) has had a large impact on how entrepreneurs think about marketing their new business.

13. See the 2009 research paper "Do friends influence purchases in a social network" by Raghuram Iyengar, Sangman Han, and Sunil Gupta.

6

We are influenced by what is around us

SOCIAL PROOF

We copy other people's behavior, especially people like us

When people are unsure about how they should act or feel, they observe the people around them. This is known as social proof. Research shows that when we observe others, our brains simulate what they are feeling.[1]

Not all social proof is conscious. As much research shows, we are also subconsciously influenced by the actions of others. We often change our behavior based on what people are doing around us, but don't realize that we're being influenced. For example, people sitting next to heavy eaters eat more. People dining alone eat less than people eating in groups. People eating with one other person eat 35 percent more than what they eat at home. People eating in a party of four eat 75 percent more.[2] If your friends are happy, you're more likely to be happy. If they smoke, you're more likely to smoke. If they are lonely, you're more likely to be lonely. Students who live with studious roommates tend to study more.[3] People are more likely to buy computers in areas where a lot of other people already own computers.[4] People buy cars based on what others around them are driving, regardless of their demographics.[5]

Social proof can be used to show people the preferred course of action or appropriate behavior. But it can also send out the wrong signals. For example, communicating that people are littering shows people that others are littering, and rather than encouraging people to stop littering, it may show that it's an acceptable behavior.[6] We may have a car we want to be proud of, but if our neighbors are not taking care of their cars, we may drop our standards to match.

Although we're influenced by a huge range of people around us, we're disproportionately influenced by people we perceive to be like us. This effect is greater when people can compare themselves to people like them: people of similar age, ethnicity, background, and ability.[7]

We are influenced by what people have done before us

When we're unsure about what to do, and can't observe other people's behavior firsthand, we're often influenced by any signs of what people have done before us. Research on amazon.com found that people don't give things objective reviews and ratings; rather, they tend to give things the same ratings as other people have given before them.[8] A high average rating makes it much more unlikely that someone will give something a one-star rating, even if that was what they intended before they saw the ratings of others.

Research by Duncan Watts found that knowing what music other people listened to had a far more powerful effect than whether or not the music was of high quality. Music people chose to listen to was the same music that people had listened to before them.[9]

> What the Music Lab experiment showed was that when individuals are influenced by what other people are doing, similar groups of people can end up behaving in very different ways.
>
> —Duncan Watts

We are influenced by the society we live in

We're not born into a neutral environment. We're born into a specific culture, a set of habits and rituals, attitudes and beliefs, that guide how we behave. We learn these unwritten rules from observing the behavior of people around us and their reactions to our behavior. For example, Eastern cultures emphasize relationships and groups while Western cultures emphasize individuals. When you show someone who grew up in an Eastern culture and someone who grew up in a Western culture the same landscape photograph, the person from the East will talk much more about the overall scene, while the person from the West will talk much more about the focal objects. From our early years, we internalize the rules of our culture, and act accordingly. We obey the law and stop our car at a red light at 4 a.m., even when no one is around, because that's what we've learned is the right behavior.[10]

Culture is an emergent system. It forms from the common actions and behaviors of many people who are reacting to other peoples' behavior. We learn what is appropriate in our culture haphazardly, depending on the experiences we have.

We are influenced by social norms

Social norms are accepted behaviors within a culture, for example, shaking hands at the end of a tennis game or walking into an elevator and turning to face the doors. Not shaking hands, or facing the back wall of an elevator, would violate the social norm, and make others uncomfortable.[11] We work hard to conform to the social norms in our culture, and we disapprove of people violating the social norms.

Social norms can vary dramatically from group to group, even within the same culture. Gossip is how groups establish social norms. We talk about other people—what they said, what they did, how they acted—and we make approving or disapproving statements. Others in the group listen, and learn how to behave in the future. People gossip, establish social norms, and gossip further to reinforce those norms.

QUICK TIPS

Showing others' behavior is a powerful way to influence people. Behavioral change precedes attitudinal change. Facebook's Open Graph shows the activity of other people, and gives people tools to undertake the same activity.

When you can't highlight the behavior of people's friends, highlight the behavior of people like them, and explicitly describe why those people are like them. Below is an example from Last.fm, which has a "Friends" tab and a "Neighbors" tab. Show what those people have done in the past.

Show what is desired behavior within a specific culture, and encourage people to reinforce those norms through interaction that spreads to their friends.

INFLUENCE WITHIN GROUPS

We are influenced by people in our group

We often change our behavior to conform to the expectations, attitudes, and behavior of our group. This can include our family, friends, workmates, or sports teammates.[7] This often happens subconsciously.

People can distinguish between members of their own group and members of another group in under 170 milliseconds.[12] Our groups define who we are, and we often act to preserve the social norms held by the group. We structure our social network around people in our groups and people outside our groups. Much of this structural thought is subconscious, and we are often negatively biased towards people outside our groups without knowing it.

We increasingly turn to others to help us make decisions

When we are uncertain about what to do, we turn to others to help us make a decision. We know that we have limited access to information as well as limited memory, so we rely on the other people in our group because we know they will have more information. We do this so often and so naturally that we sometimes turn to others even when the answer is obvious.[13]

When we're faced with an increasing number of choices, we find it much harder to make a decision. The development of the web means that our access to information is increasing exponentially. If Wikipedia were printed, it would be over two million pages long, and would take more than a lifetime to read.

In a world of exponentially increasing information, decisions will be harder because our capacity for memory will remain the same. With exponentially increasing information, and limited capacity for memory, we will increasingly turn to others to help us decide.

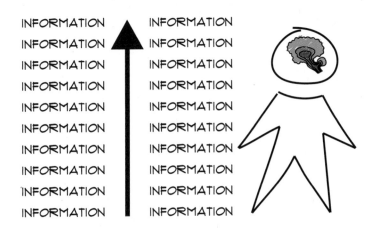

Since the creation of the web, the amount of information accessible to us is increasing exponentially, but our capacity for memory has taken millions of years to evolve and won't change within our lifetime.

Not everyone in a group is equal

We have unique relationships with the people in our life and are closer to some than others. Even in the tightest of groups, there are conversations between a subset of members that happen outside the main conversation. We trust the opinion of some of our friends on one topic and others on a different topic. Sometimes we trust the opinion of our closest friends, even though they may not be the most knowledgeable in our group about a topic.

As we increase our reliance on our social networks to make decisions, we won't turn to strangers, nor will we turn to recognized experts. Instead we will turn to the same people we have been genetically trained to turn to for help—the people we're emotionally closest to.

Groups can make better decisions than individuals

Under the right conditions, groups are often better than individuals at making decisions. James Surowiecki defined four criteria necessary for a group decision to be accurate[14]:

· People's judgments need to be independent, and not influenced by the other group members.

· People should have a diverse range of opinions, even if they are just multiple interpretations of the facts.

· People should be able to draw on local or specialized knowledge.

· All group members' opinions need to be aggregated.

Research by Bahador Bahrami showed that pairs perform better than individuals as long as they discuss what they saw and talk about how confident they are in the observations that they disagree about.[15] Sometimes, a group of non-experts is better than an individual expert at predicting outcomes in the expert's field, for example, predicting stock market performance.

QUICK TIPS

The next great challenge on the social web is to understand who we trust about what. We can now see the activity of the people in our network, but these people are not equal. In the example below, I may trust Sam's taste in music more than Jenna's, or Adam's taste in music more than Justin's.

Remember that people don't trust the opinions of the people that are objectively placed to give advice. They trust their closest friends and family, and those are the relationships that we need to design around.

INFLUENCE WITHIN OUR EXTENDED NETWORK

Our social network defines how information and influence spread

It's hard for us to imagine what our social network looks like, but it influences almost everything we do, from the people we meet, to the places we go, to the things we do, to the things we buy.

We know our family and friends, and we know some of *their* friends, but we don't know all the people they are connected to or which of them know each other. In a group of just 10 people, there are approximately 50 possible relationships. In a group of 100 people, there are approximately 5,000 possible relationships. Among the people we know, our decisions to meet them, pass on information to them, or interact with them in any other way are based on all the interactions we've had together in the past, which can be many thousands.

We are only influenced by people up to three degrees away

We briefly covered the "Three Degrees of Influence" rule in Chapter 3. Researchers Nicholas Christakis and James Fowler studied data collected from 5,000 people over a 20-year period. They found that your friends' friends' friends, usually people you don't know, can have a dramatic impact on your behavior and the decisions you make.[3] If your friend's friend's friend does something, that influences your friend's friend, which influences your friend, which influences you. They found this across many behaviors, including weight loss and quitting smoking. Remarkably, they found that the level of influence almost completely disappears once you go beyond three degrees, that is, your friends' friends' friends. This can have a profound effect on how information spreads.

HOW EXPERTS EXERT INFLUENCE

Our trusted experts are often people we know

When deciding what to do, we often turn to people we see as experts in their domain. We trust doctors to give us credible medical advice. We trust mechanics to give us advice on our car. But even in one of these circumstances, the strength of our relationship with the expert plays a role. Research by Forrester found that cancer patients trust their local care physician more than world renowned cancer treatment centers, and in most cases, the patient had known their local care physician for years.[16]

We overrate the advice of experts

Psychologist Philip Tetlock conducted numerous studies to test the accuracy of advice from experts in the fields of journalism and politics. He quantified over 82,000 predictions and found that the journalism experts tended to perform slightly worse than picking answers at random. Political experts didn't fare much better. They slightly outperformed random chance, but did not perform as well as a basic statistical model. In fact, they actually performed slightly better at predicting things *outside* their area of expertise, and 80 percent of their predictions were wrong. Studies in finance also show that only 20 percent of investment bankers outperform the stock market.[17]

We overestimate what we know

Sometimes we consider ourselves as experts, even though we don't know as much as we think we know. Research by Russo and Schoemaker asked managers in the advertising industry questions about their domain. Participants were correct 61 percent of the time, but were confident that they were correct 90 percent of the time. Russo and Schoemaker studied fields outside of advertising and across 2,000 people found that 99 percent of people overestimated their success rate.[18] Ironically, the reason for this overconfidence is having too much information. When we have too much information at our disposal, we lose track of which facts are most important, we draw correlations between sets of data when they are just coincidences, and we use the information at our disposal to rationalize our answers. In fact, many research studies have shown that strangers are almost as good at predicting our behavior as we are ourselves.[19]

QUICK TIPS

Consider how you use "experts" in your marketing campaigns. The trusted expert may not be the best in their field, but instead they may simply be the closest credible person.

Because we overrate the advice of experts, using experts in marketing campaigns can lead to over-promising and under-delivering, which can damage longer-term credibility with the brand.

SUMMARY

Our culture is a set of habits and rituals, attitudes and beliefs, that guide how we behave. They are unwritten rules that we learn from observing people around us as well as from people's reactions to our behavior. One aspect of our culture is the social norms associated with that culture. We work hard to conform to the social norms in our culture.

When people are unsure about how they should act, they observe the behavior of the people around them and act in a consistent manner. People in our group, and people we perceive to be like us, disproportionately influence us. We often change our behavior to conform to the expectations, attitudes, and behavior of our group.

We overrate the advice of experts. Random strangers can often outperform experts.

FURTHER READING

1. See the Wikipedia article titled *Mirror Neuron* for an introduction and further reading.

2. See Richard Thaler and Cass Sunstein's book *Nudge: Improving Decisions About Health, Wealth, and Happiness* (Yale University Press, 2008).

3. In their book *Connected* (Little, Brown, 2009), Nicholas Christakis and James Fowler describe how people are influenced by social proof.

4. See the 2002 research paper "Evidence on learning and network externalities in the diffusion of home computers" by Austan Goolsbee and Peter Klenow.

5. See the 2003 research paper "Modeling interdependent consumer preferences" by Sha Yang and Greg Allenby.

6. This example is from Robert Cialdini. For more examples of social proof see the 2007 research paper "Using social norms as a lever of social influence" by Cialdini and Goldstein.

7. See the principle of similarity described in B. J. Fogg's book *Persuasive Technology* (Morgan Kaufmann, 2003).

8. See the 2009 research paper "Analysis of social influence in online book reviews" by Patty Sakunkoo and Nathan Sakunkoo.

9. See three research papers published by Duncan Watts and Matthew Salganik. The earliest is the 2006 paper "Experimental study of inequality and unpredictability in an artificial cultural market," followed by the 2008 paper "Leading the herd astray: An experimental study of self-fulfilling prophecies in an artificial cultural market," and finally the 2009 paper "Web-based experiments for the study of collective social dynamics in cultural markets."

10. This example is from Dan Ariely's book *Predictably Irrational: The Hidden Forces That Shape Our Decisions* (Harper Perennial, 2008).

11. See the Wikipedia article on *Social Norms* for more information.

12. See the 2010 poster presentation "N170 responses to faces predict implicit ingroup favoritism" by Kyle Ratner and David Amodio.

13. See the work of Herbert Simon and the Wikipedia article on *Bounded Rationality*.

14. See James Surowiecki's book *The Wisdom of Crowds* (Anchor, 2005).

15. See the 2010 research paper "Optimally interacting minds" by Bahrami and others.

16. Data from the NCCN private community of cancer patients as described in *Groundswell*, a book by Charlene Li and Josh Bernoff (Harvard Business Press, 2008).

17. See Philip Tetlock's book *Expert Political Judgment: How Good Is It? How Can We Know*? (Princeton University Press, 2006).

18. See Russo and Schoemaker's book *Winning Decisions: Getting It Right the First Time* (Crown Business, 2001).

19. See Timothy Wilson's book *Strangers to Ourselves: Discovering the Adaptive Unconscious* (Harvard University Press, 2004).

7
How our brain influences us

WE ARE NOT RATIONAL THINKERS

The end of reductive thinking

Anyone who needs to capture people's interest and attention needs to know how the brain works. Ever since the ancient Greeks, we have assumed that humans are rational, that we weigh the pros and cons in any given situation, and make rational choices based on the facts available to us. But we are now learning that this is not how the brain works.

We have spent the past few hundred years pulling things apart in order to understand how they work. This was based on the idea that we are rational, logical thinkers, and could figure out complex systems by finding all their components. In many areas of science, we have managed to pull apart all the components, yet we are still not much closer to understanding how the system works. We have been examining systems that emerge from combinations of simple interactions, and although we can see the interactions, we can't yet understand how all these interactions relate to one another.[1] Our social network is an emergent system—we can see the people but we can't see all the relationships. Society is an emergent system. Our brain is an emergent system. If we want to understand how people influence each other and make decisions, we must focus on the relationships between components, rather than the components themselves.

We rely on the emotional brain

We make a tiny minority of decisions with our rational brain. We make almost all of our decisions using our emotional brain. When trying to decide between multiple choices, we don't carefully weigh up the options; rather, we use mental shortcuts, many of which are inaccurate and misleading.

Our conscious (rational) brain has very limited processing capabilities and relies on our nonconscious (emotional) brain to tell us what to do. In any given decision, our nonconscious brain does an incredible amount of invisible analysis and generates a *feeling* that it sends to our conscious brain. Our conscious brain then uses this feeling to make a decision. Reason is dependent on emotion.

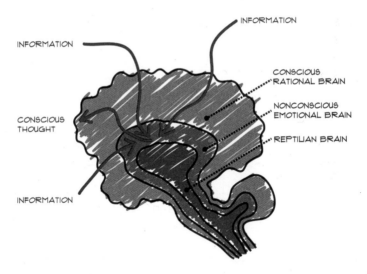

Vast amounts of information are analyzed by our nonconscious brain and communicated to our conscious brain.

This critical shift in understanding changes how we must think about consumer behavior. The classic sales funnel is based on a view of humans as rational thinkers, making rational decisions as they move down through the funnel. But we now know that that is simply not true. Over the past few hundred years, we have overestimated the power and importance of the conscious brain. Most behavior is driven by the nonconscious brain, which we can't access. Most of us can't explain why we do what we do, why we decide what we decide, or how we will behave in the future. This casts a lot of questions over what we infer about consumer behavior from what people tell us in research studies.

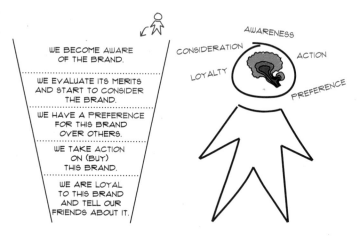

We think about consumer behavior as a linear process (left), when in fact it's nonlinear and chaotic (right). Often we take action before having a preference, or reconsider our options after having a strong preference.

We experience the world through patterns

As we go through life, we use our unique experiences and perceptions to build patterns of how the world works. We store these patterns as neural networks in the brain. Because we all have unique experiences, our patterns are different. These patterns have a huge influence over our behavior, and over how much attention we pay to different things when making decisions.

Our brains have evolved to constantly scan our environment and ensure that nothing life threatening is present, just as they did hundreds of thousands of years ago on the African savannah. Because of this, new or unexpected things—things that don't fit into the expected pattern—capture our attention.[2] Neuroscience studies have shown that our brains not only look for the unexpected, they crave the unexpected.[3]

Our brain is constantly looking for patterns because it finds it hard to deal with the idea that some things are random. We see random cloud formations and think we're seeing objects. We see a basketball player score multiple shots in a row and think they are on a "hot streak" ("hot streaks" don't actually exist). Our brains look for patterns and look to see if those patterns match any patterns already stored in memory. When the patterns match, the neural networks get deeper, and our views become more entrenched. When they don't match, the brain recalibrates and stores new patterns.

Brains are built to generate predictions. The ability to predict is the foundation of problem-solving. The neocortex stores memories and uses them to make predictions about what will happen next. It then observes what actually happens, and measures and records the difference. When we solve problems, our brain doesn't compute the answer, it retrieves the solutions from memory.[4] Our dynamic and constantly adjusting emotions are not hard-wired instincts, they are messages from our unconscious. The vast majority of our brain's predictions happen outside of our awareness.

QUICK TIPS

The classic marketing/sales funnel is an incredibly useful tool to focus conversations on specific aspects of marketing activity. However, it's not a good model for talking about consumer behavior because it makes many incorrect assumptions. A better model for consumer behavior is our social network structure model, illustrated below.

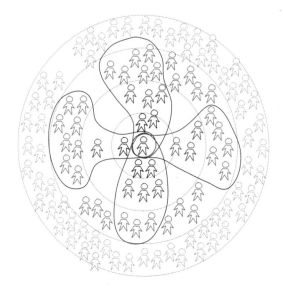

Although unexpected things get our attention, this is not a good reason to practice interruption marketing. Unexpected is more often a negative experience, and even if we all created positive unexpected interruptions, when everyone tries to get people's attention, no one gets their attention.

MOST OF OUR BEHAVIOR IS DRIVEN BY OUR NONCONSCIOUS BRAIN

Our conscious brains are not designed to process huge amounts of information

Our brain is split into three parts. The conscious brain is the only part we can directly access. The nonconscious brain has two components: our midbrain processes emotions and drives most of our behavior, and our old brain keeps us alive by keeping our heart beating and our lungs breathing.

Because we live in an information rich world, our brains are designed to take conscious information and turn it into unconscious information. For example, when learning to drive a car, you have to consciously think about every action. But once you learn how to do it, it becomes automatic and your nonconscious brain does the job for you. This leaves our conscious brain to think about other things while we drive.[5]

Although our brain has limited processing capacity, we've built a world with more communication than anyone can process. Too many choices, too many alternatives, too much information— and the problem is getting worse. We've seen that the amount of information accessible to us is increasing exponentially. Because our conscious brain can't handle all this information, it creates shortcuts, many of which mislead us.

We give more weight to information that we're conscious of, but our nonconscious brain has over 200,000 times more processing capacity than our conscious brain.[5] Marketers must consider the role of the nonconscious brain in decision-making. The nonconscious brain is deeply empirical. It learns from its past experiences and mistakes. The conscious brain receives its input from the nonconscious brain and relies on short-term memory, whereas the nonconscious brain relies on its vast memory system for decisions.

The processing capacity of the conscious brain is the single dot on the left. There are 20,000 dots in the grid on the right. Imagine that times *ten* to give you an idea of how much more powerful the nonconscious brain is. Our conscious mind can only access the single dot on the left.

Much social influence is processed by our nonconscious brain. We observe others' behavior and pick up on their subtle cues about what is appropriate, without consciously realizing that we have altered our own behavior. Marketers can't attempt to understand social behavior in isolation. If they want to understand individual action, they need to conduct consumer research by trying to understand the influence of the network in which people live.

Our nonconscious brain makes most of our decisions

When we need to make a decision, the nonconscious brain assesses the alternatives, generates a positive or negative feeling based on its conclusion, and sends that feeling to the conscious brain. This is why we're drawn more to some things than to others. Our nonconscious brain has already completed a detailed analysis and advised us on what to do—from complex purchase decisions like buying a car to mundane ones like choosing breakfast cereal. By the time our conscious brain swings into action, our nonconscious brain has already analyzed the thousands of variables before it, like how expensive each cereal is, how healthy each is, whether we recognize them, whether we've had them before, and if so what we thought of them, whether we've seen an ad for the cereal, what message we took away from it, and whether we believed what it had to say. Even the smallest, most mundane purchase decisions arise from a deep nonconscious analysis. When consumer goods companies like Procter & Gamble run a TV ad in a specific town and watch the subsequent sales of the advertised product go up in the local Wal-Mart, it's because the TV ads seeded reminders with the nonconscious brain, not with the conscious brain.

The nonconscious brain can detect patterns and knows what to do long before the conscious brain does. In one experiment, card players were able to choose cards from one of four decks. Two of the decks were intentionally bad, with much poorer cards. People started to avoid the bad decks long before they became consciously aware that there was any difference between the decks.[2]

Our nonconscious brain is often better at making decisions than our conscious brain

When there are few choices and few variables, the conscious brain makes better choices. However, our world is being filled with more variables and more choices. When things aren't clear, when there are many incoming signals, our nonconscious brain makes better decisions.

Research into how people purchase cars found that people who used their conscious brain chose the best car 25 percent of the time, whereas people who used their nonconscious brain chose the best car 60 percent of the time. In other words, people using their rational, conscious brain made a poor choice more often than if they used their nonconscious brain, and more often than if their car was chosen at random.[5] There are too many variables in choosing a car for the rational conscious brain to process, so it chooses a subset of variables to base its decision on. But it usually picks variables that aren't very important, like the color of the seats. Research has shown that the conscious brain can only process fewer than ten variables (some studies conclude that it's only four variables), much less than the variables present in most decisions. People often make better decisions after looking at a choice and making an immediate decision (when their emotional nonconscious brain decides) than when they study the problem over days, weeks, or months (when their rational conscious brain decides).[6]

OUR MEMORY IS HIGHLY UNRELIABLE

Our most frequent recollections are the least accurate

As we recall memories, we remake them. Every time we remake them, we add fictional details to fill the missing gaps. Therefore, the more we remember something, the less accurate the memory becomes.

We also change our memories as time passes. In one study, while leaving the movie theater people thought that the movie they just watched was particularly good. The next day after having read a negative movie review, their recollection was that as they left the theater the day before they did not like the movie.[6]

People remember key relationships, not details

Our brain couldn't possibly store all the details of everything that we experience. It's more important to store the relationships between things over time. This is brain efficiency honed over millions of years of evolution. The brain doesn't care about accuracy or detail. It is only interested in remembering things it thinks will help us make decisions in the future.

Our brain remembers and stores relationships between things, independent of the details. When it needs to remember details, it makes information up out of thin air to fill the gaps it left when it stored the memory. It pulls this information from all our other memories—past experiences, cultural norms, imagined outcomes—and fills in whatever detail it needs to create a seamless story.[7] Our memories can be highly inaccurate.

Many research studies have observed people's behavior and then asked them to recap what they did. Depending on the study, some asked participants to recap immediately afterward, some after a day, some after a week, some after a month. What these studies consistently show is that we elaborate on details and describe events that never happened, regardless of the gap in time after the behavior. We have no conscious awareness that we fabricated these details; our nonconscious brain did it to fill the gaps in knowledge. In one study, people were secretly filmed in a store, and interviewed after they had passed through the register. Nine out of ten people remembered holding both the brand they bought *and* a competitor brand in their hands while comparing them; however, the recorded film showed that fewer than one in ten people actually held both brands.[8]

We can only remember a small amount at a time, in sequence

Because we have so many memories stored in our heads, we can only recall a small number of them at any one time, and we can only recall them in the sequence that we remembered them. Try saying the alphabet backwards. Or reciting the months of the year backwards. Or your phone number backwards. Try singing a song backwards, or even reciting the lyrics in a different sequence than the original, like starting with the third verse.

We often can't remember large things, like a full song. We can only remember parts of the song, but because we stored it in sequence, remembering the start makes the rest of the song come flooding back.[4] Think about trying to retell a story or a joke. It's often hard to remember how it starts, but once you remember the start, it's easy to remember the rest.

QUICK TIPS

Create marketing and advertising content that relies on people remembering relationships and not details, and that is structured in a sequence.

We need to understand the limitations on memory when interpreting consumer research results. People can't accurately remember what they did and why they did it. Quantitative methods that rely on memory need to be conducted in conjunction with *real-time* qualitative techniques such as in-person observations and diary studies.

SUMMARY

If you want to understand how to influence people, you need to understand relationships, and not the component parts of people's behavior.

We have very limited processing capabilities and make a tiny minority of decisions with our rational brain. The classic sales funnel is based on humans as rational thinkers, but we now know that our decisions are based on emotions, not rational thinking.

Over the past few hundred years, we have overestimated the power and importance of our rational, conscious brain. Most of our behavior is driven by our emotional nonconscious brain, which we can't access. Our brains are not designed to consciously process huge amounts of information, yet that is the world we have built around us.

Marketers need to think about the role of the nonconscious brain. By the time your conscious brain swings into action, your nonconscious brain has already analyzed the thousands of variables before it. When things aren't clear, when there are many incoming signals, our nonconscious brain makes much better decisions.

Our brain remembers and stores relationships between things, independent of the details. This is because it couldn't possibly store all the details of everything that we experience. When it needs to remember details, it makes information up out of thin air to fill the gaps it left when it stored the memory.

FURTHER READING

1. For more details on emergence, see the Wikipedia article of the same name, and Steven Johnson's book *Emergence: The Connected Lives of Ants, Brains, Cities, and Software* (Scribner, 2002).

2. For more on brain patterns, see Susan Weinschenk's book *100 Things Every Designer Needs to Know About People* (New Riders Press, 2011).

3. See the 2001 research paper "Predictability modulates human brain response to reward" by Gregory Berns and others.

4. For more information about the memory-prediction framework of the brain, see the book *On Intelligence* by Jeff Hawkins (Times Books, 2004).

5. See the research work done by Ap Dijksterhuis. Start with the 2009 research paper "The rational unconscious: Conscious versus unconscious thought in complex consumer choice."

6. See the 2011 research paper "Should I go with my gut? Investigating the benefits of emotion-focused decision making" by researchers at DePaul University, and the 2006 article "A theory of unconscious thought" by Ap Dijksterhuis and Loran Nordgren. Other studies have concluded that although the nonconscious brain is incredibly powerful, its influence has been overblown. For this alternative viewpoint, see the article "Can the unconscious outperform the conscious mind?" on *PsyBlog*.

7. For a detailed look at how our memories are often part truth, part fabrication, see Daniel Gilbert's book *Stumbling on Happiness* (Knopf, 2006).

8. Based on a research study cited in Kevin Hogan's book *The Science of Influence: How to Get Anyone to Say "Yes" in 8 Minutes or Less!* (Wiley, 2010).

8

How our biases influence us

OTHER PEOPLE BIAS US

The actions of others influence our behavior

If someone gives us something, we have a natural desire to give something in return at some point in the future. This is one of the most powerful tactics for persuading people to do something, as the desire sticks with people over time. We never forget that "we owe them one."

When other people ask us to do something, and we respect them or think that they have our best interests at heart, we are strongly motivated to fulfill their request regardless of whether the outcome will be positive or negative for us.

Having common ground biases us toward others

People who are similar to us in areas like personality, age, race, and preferences, and share the same values and beliefs, whether we know them or not, usually have a much greater influence over us than people not like us. Even the smallest amount of common ground can change how much someone can influence us, for example, following the same sports team or sharing the same hometown.

We remain consistent with past behavior when others see us act

Once we decide something, we tend to stick to that decision, even when faced with overwhelming evidence to the contrary. This is true for things we say, things we write down, and things we do. Even if the decision turns out not to be in our best interests, we still stick with that decision to be consistent with our past decisions. In fact, research has shown that when we receive new information, we analyze and store it in ways that reinforce what we already think.[1]

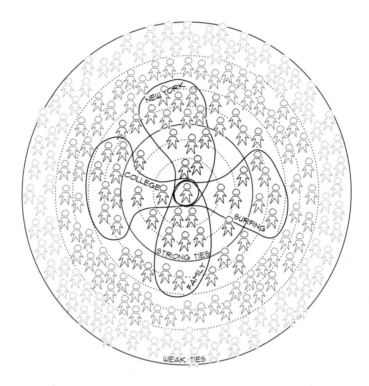

Our behavior is influenced by who saw us act. We may act one way with one group, forcing us to act consistently when with them in the future, whereas we may act differently with another group. These subtle differences in behavior with our different groups lead to awkward interactions when these groups come together, for example, at weddings and birthday parties.

When we make impulse decisions, we tend to stand by them and rationalize them to others, rather than accept that they may not have been the best decisions.

Because of our desire for consistency with past actions, we are more open to ideas when they fit with our preexisting beliefs. It makes it easier for us to accept the new idea.

OUR PERCEPTION OF VALUE BIASES US

We want more information and more choices than we can actually process

We think that more choice means more freedom. But when faced with many choices, people often can't make a decision and walk away from all the choices. In one study, researchers set up a jam stand in a supermarket. In one version, they had 24 choices of jam, and in the other they had 6 choices. When there were 24 choices, 60 percent of people who passed would stop and look, but only 3 percent would make a purchase. When there were 6 choices, only 40 percent of people who passed would stop and look, but 30 percent would make a purchase. The larger number of choices were good for getting people's attention, but were ultimately far worse for sales.[2] In a study on how people select pension funds, when 95 funds were offered, about 60 percent of people participated, but when only 2 funds were offered, the rate of participation jumped to 75 percent.[3] When Procter & Gamble reduced the number of Head & Shoulders products from 26 to 15, they saw a 10 percent increase in sales.[4] Often it is better to offer fewer choices.

Although we want more information, when we have two or more conflicting ideas in our head, we become overwhelmed. This is known as cognitive dissonance and we often experience it when shopping. When this happens, we often pick the option that matches our current beliefs, and disregard all other options without evaluating them properly. When we buy things, in particular expensive things, we often feel discomfort after the purchase because we're not sure if the purchase was a good decision. Instead of returning the item, we're much more likely to reduce the dissonance by telling everyone how great the purchase was, and convincing ourselves in the process.

We're overly concerned with losing what we already have

Most people will do far more to avoid losing what they already have than they will do to gain something new of equal value. This is part of a broader pattern called negativity bias, which shows that people feel more strongly about bad outcomes than good outcomes.

Our tendency to avoid loss is why people respond so positively to things that are free and perceive them to be much more valuable than they really are. When we buy or exchange to acquire things, there is loss associated with it, but when we receive things that are free, there is no risk that we're losing something, and so it gives us positive emotions.[5]

We overvalue immediate gains

As well as avoiding loss, we tend to overvalue immediate gains, and overlook what we might gain or lose in the future. We will decide on a guaranteed thing because it's available now, even when a greater gain is available after a wait. We do this because we're trying to avoid future risk. It's hardcoded into our brain. Research has shown that offering people a smaller immediate gain activated different neural systems in the brain than did offering them a larger gain in two to four weeks.[6]

QUICK TIPS

Almost all of us could look at what our business offers and conclude that there are too many options. Reduce people's choices. When you add a new product line, remove an older one. Many of the most successful brands sell a very small number of products. For example, Apple basically sells only four things: MacBooks, iMacs, iPads, and iPhones.

Reduce any perceived loss in having to interact with your brand. Make people feel like they are getting something from you for free, and that they are getting it now. For example, Pedigree gave away one free meal to a dog in a shelter every time someone *liked* their Facebook page. They built a community of over one million people (and gave away over one million dog meals) because this community felt that they got something meaningful for free.

OUR HABITS BIAS US

People's habits are hard to change

We're wired to avoid trying new things. When we're presented with information that opposes what we already do or believe, our natural reaction is to deny the new information rather than change our behavior or belief. Our brain often ignores the competing information. In fact, we actively look for information that confirms our beliefs and don't look for information that opposes our beliefs. This is why we have partisan bias in politics, despite the abundance of information on both sides.

We all have learned behaviors and perceptions that we repeat and reinforce. To have people try your product often involves breaking an existing habit—buy a different brand, shop in a different store, visit a different website. Recent research has shown that it takes about 5 days of daily repeated action for people to form a new habit. Without daily repetition, it can take from 18 to over 250 days depending on how complex the new behavior is.[7] The hard part is motivating people to start doing something new in the first place.

The time when we're most open to trying something new is when we're happy. When we're sad or scared we want what's familiar and will avoid what's new.[8]

How to change people's habits

We often use advertising to try to persuade people that there are better alternatives to what they currently do. Yet, presenting them with evidence that what they currently do is a bad choice is one of the worst ways to change people's behavior or attitude. At best, this has little influence, as we automatically ignore information counter to our beliefs. At worst, the conflicting evidence brings about cognitive dissonance, and because we don't like to hold opposing views in our head, we become *more* ingrained in what we believed before.

It's incredibly hard to change people's attitudes. It's much easier to invoke behavioral change first, and then attitudinal change later. Changes in behavior almost always lead to changes in attitude. But before people will change their behavior, they have to be ready to try something new. There are three primary ways of encouraging people to change their behavior: [9]

1. Change people's environment; this is the most powerful way to effect change. Environment stimulates specific behaviors so it's much easier to try something new in a new environment.

2. Increase the benefit relative to the cost of a new behavior. People seek to minimize costs and maximize benefits. Minimizing costs translates to breaking things down into small tasks, making the new behavior easier to perform, resulting in maximized benefits. Performing easier things makes them more likely to be repeated, which will lead to a new habit forming.

3. Ensure that people observe others doing the desired behavior and then see others being rewarded for it. We learn new behaviors by observing the people around us.

QUICK TIPS

Don't try to persuade people that their current behavior is bad. Try to motivate behavioral change, and attitudinal change will follow. There are many ways to motivate behavioral change without requiring people to part with their money. The best way to start is with lightweight actions that are easily repeatable, and social networks like Facebook are ideal for this. It takes seconds for people to like or comment on a post you make, vote on a poll you run, or interact with an app you build. Their friends observe all these actions, and our desire for consistency ensures that their new behavior will likely be continued in the future.

ENVIRONMENTAL CUES BIAS US

We are influenced by the cues that surround us

Many research studies have shown that we can influence people's behavior by cueing them with a specific perception. This is called priming and can be done with words, sounds, or by things in people's environment. In one study, people who were primed with words related to being elderly walked away from the researchers more slowly than a control group who were not primed.[10] In another study, people who were primed with rude words interrupted others almost twice as fast as people primed with polite words.[10] People who vote in a school building are much more likely to support tax increases to fund education.[11] People are much more likely to vote for the first candidate on the ballot than someone in the middle or at the end because they are primed to think of a list of people as a leaderboard.

We are influenced by how things are presented

Every decision we make is framed in a certain context and this framing can radically change our perceptions and behavior. In one research study, people who were given two glasses of the same wine to taste but were told that one was a very expensive wine and one was a cheap wine, not only preferred the "more expensive" wine but the "more expensive" wine made their brains more excited.[12] Their brain responded to the *price* of the wine rather than the wine itself. People are much more likely to buy meat that is labeled 85 pecent lean than meat that is labeled 15 percent fat, even though they are the same thing. Twice as many people opt for surgery when there is an 80 percent chance of surviving versus a 20 percent chance of dying.[13] When one group of people were asked how many murders occur every year in Detroit, and another group were asked how many murders occur in Michigan, the average guesses were 200 in Detroit and 100 in Michigan, yet Detroit is a city within the state of Michigan.

We don't process things in isolation

When we make a decision, we don't think about things in isolation, we compare them to other things. Often, we rely too much on one comparison and use that as an anchor for future decision making. We also only compare things which are *easy* to compare, even though they may not be the most important things to compare. For example, we compare things that are near to each other in space or time. Decision researcher Itamar Simonson found that people tend to avoid extremes and make choices that are intermediate between what they need at a minimum and what they can possibly spend at a maximum.[14]

QUICK TIPS

There are many great books on how to use priming, framing, and anchoring in marketing campaigns. The reason it's important to understand them in the context of this book is because leveraging these behavior patterns will become more important as the amount of information we are exposed to continues to increase. One new approach to take is to think about how the published online activities of people's friends can prime their behavior, frame their decisions, and influence what they compare your brand to.

SUMMARY

Once we decide something, we tend to stick to that decision, even when faced with overwhelming evidence to the contrary. Our desire for consistency makes us less open to new ideas unless they fit with our pre-existing beliefs.

People who are similar to us in areas like personality, age, race, and preferences, and share the same values and beliefs, usually have a much greater influence over us than people not like us.

People want more information and more choices than they can actually process despite the fact that two or more conflicting ideas in our head is overwhelming. When this happens, we either walk away from all choices, or pick the option that matches our current beliefs without evaluating alternatives.

Many research studies have shown that we can influence people's behavior by cueing them with a specific perception, framing a situation in a certain light, and influencing what we compare things to.

We're wired to avoid trying new things. When people are presented with information that opposes what they already believe, their natural reaction is to deny the new information rather than change their belief.

It's much easier to invoke behavioral change first, and attitudinal change later. You can motivate behavioral change by changing people's environments, breaking down requests into much smaller requests, and ensuring people see others doing the desired behavior.

FURTHER READING

1. This is known as confirmation bias. See Raymond Nickerson's 1998 paper "Confirmation bias: A ubiquitous phenomenon in many guises."

2. See the 2000 research paper "When choice is demotivating: Can one desire too much of a good thing?" by Sheena Iyengar and Mark Lepper.

3. See the 2004 research paper "How much choice is too much? Contributions to 401(k) retirement plans" by Iyengar, Jiang, and Huberman.

4. See the 1997 *Philadelphia Inquirer* article "Too many choices? Firms cut back on new products" by E. Osnos.

5. For further reading on decision biases, see Dan Ariely's book *Predictably Irrational* (HarperCollins, 2008).

6. For more reading on neuroscience research on temptation, see the work of Jonathan Cohen, in particular his 2005 research paper "The vulcanization of the human brain: A neural perspective on interactions between cognition and emotion."

7. For research on how long it takes to form habits, see the 2010 research paper "How are habits formed: Modelling habit formation in the real world" by researchers at University College London.

8. Marieke De Vries has conducted multiple studies into the relationship between happiness and decision making. For starters, see her 2010 research paper "Mood effects on dominated choices: Positive mood induces departures from logical rules."

9. For more information on how observing others affects our behavior, see the Wikipedia article on *Social cognitive theory*.

10. See the 1996 article "Automaticity of social behavior: Direct effects of trait construct and stereotype activation on action" by researchers at New York University.

11. See the 2008 research paper "Can where people vote influence how they vote? The influence of polling location type on voting behavior" by researchers at Stanford.

12. See the 2007 research paper "Marketing actions can modulate neural representations of experienced pleasantness" by researchers at Caltech and Stanford.

13. These examples are taken from Jonah Lehrer's book *How We Decide* (Houghton Mifflin, 2009).

14. Find out more on Itamar Simonson's research in the 1993 article "Get closer to your customers by understanding how they make choices."

9

Marketing and advertising on the social web

THE PROBLEMS FACING INTERRUPTION MARKETING

Interruption marketing is a race to the bottom

For the past 100 years, marketers have mostly relied on interruption marketing to get their message across, and viewed each new technology as a new way to interrupt people from what they were currently doing to get them to consume their message instead. Our TV programs are interrupted by ads. Our concentration while driving is interrupted by ads. Our magazine stories are interrupted by ads. Our web experiences are interrupted by ads.

There are two main problems with interruption marketing. The first is that it is a terrible experience for people. For every welcome interruption, there are dozens of unwelcome interruptions. In social settings we don't like it when other people interrupt our conversations, and research has shown that we don't like it when marketers do it either. The second problem with interruption marketing is that people have a limited amount of time and attention. Because more and more marketers are vying for this attention, fewer and fewer of them are heard. Instead, we ignore everything, and walk away from all the choices.

Increasing frequency makes the problem worse

Both of these problems are becoming worse. We are being bombarded by more and more competing information, yet our capacity for processing and remembering this information remains the same. The increased competition for that attention means marketers must increase the frequency of their communication, exacerbating the problem. We're seeing advertising appear in more and more unusual places. No one owns this problem and so it gets worse and worse.[1] Interruption marketing is a race to the bottom.

The most common way for marketers to increase their chances of being noticed is to increase the frequency of their campaigns. More people are likely to notice it, but it creates immense volumes of noise. On average, you need to run an ad 27 times before someone remembers it: Only one out of every nine ads is noticed, and people need to see the ad three times to remember it, so it takes 27 impressions for it to sink in.[2]

People no longer trust marketers

One clear trend over the past 50 years is that people are more wary of advertising, and trust businesses less than they used to.[3] In fact, this is so prevalent that researcher Dan Ariely has found that mistrust in marketing information negatively colors our entire perception of a product, even when we have direct experience to the contrary. He conducted a series of experiments that asked people if statements such as "the sun is yellow" were true. A hundred percent of participants agreed. However, when a business such as Procter & Gamble, or the Democratic Party, was associated with issuing the statement, people started to suspect how truthful the statements were. They replied that the sun is sometimes white and has red spots on the surface so isn't really yellow. Ariely conducted similar experiments with actual products and their marketing campaigns. He found that because of their mistrust, people couldn't even identify obviously correct statements in the marketing material.[4]

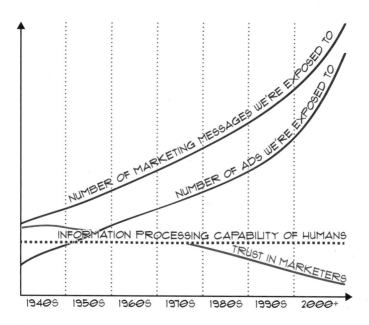

NUMBER OF MARKETING MESSAGES WE'RE EXPOSED TO

NUMBER OF ADS WE'RE EXPOSED TO

INFORMATION PROCESSING CAPABILITY OF HUMANS

TRUST IN MARKETERS

1940S 1950S 1960S 1970S 1980S 1990S 2000+

A directional graph to illustrate the problems. Before television advertising took off in the 1950s, there was a manageable amount of brand messages in our world. But as the number of these messages increased, it surpassed what our brain could process. As the number grew even larger, people found it harder and harder to know what to trust.

QUICK TIPS

The exponential increase in information brought about by the development of the web has changed the world of marketing. Brands that continue to predominantly practice interruption marketing will start to suffer. The factors that determine what people pay attention to have changed, and the era of successfully interrupting people to gain their attention is over.

THE RISE OF PERMISSION MARKETING AND WORD OF MOUTH

Increasing the reach of advertising campaigns will no longer work

Most advertisement campaigns are focused on how many people can be reached with their message. Often, basic targeting happens, which is in line with how the marketers have positioned the product. But in many cases, the advertising is shown mostly to people who have no interest in, or need for, the product or brand being advertised. The approach is that if we show the message to enough people enough times, some of it will stick. The focus on reach using interruption advertising is simply a means to an end. It's the solution to not knowing who will be interested in seeing your ad. Instead, the goal should be that enough people will absorb and believe in your message to increase sales and keep the business profitable, rather than to *reach* as many people as possible, or even a certain number of people.

The tactic of increasing reach by interruption advertising campaigns is no longer feasible. Because of the exponential increase in the amount of information accessible to us, and the increase in the number of marketing messages we receive each day, increasing reach will no longer have much impact.

We need to move away from interruption models, and towards permission models. We should build campaigns by asking people whether they are interested in hearing from us. We then communicate with these people, and rely on them telling their friends to get us the desired reach.

Permission marketing

Permission marketing happens when people give marketers permission to send them messages. Clicking the Like button on a brand's Facebook page is an example of permission marketing. People click Like because they are interested in the brand, and in doing so they give the marketer permission to place posts in their News Feed. This is where it gets interesting. When people see those posts, they are much more likely to click Like or to comment on the post than if they had been interrupted by the marketer. Their interaction with the brand is then shown in their friends' News Feed. So with permission marketing, you're not only reaching people interested in your brand, but you're also reaching their friends.

The amount of permission can increase over time. As the relationship builds between the marketer and potential customer and people start to trust the marketer, they give more permission to access personal data, which helps the marketer create more relevant content. It is a positive, reciprocal relationship based on mutual trust.

People *Like* businesses that they are interested in hearing from.

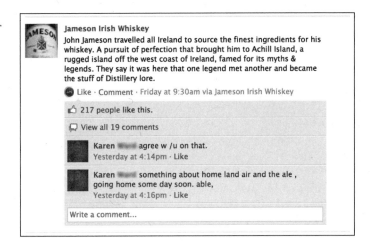

That business can then post content to their page, which can show up in the News Feed of their fans. This content tends to be more conversational in nature than traditional advertising copy, which helps to build trust in the brand.

Permission marketing and word of mouth

As we saw with the Facebook News Feed, permission marketing becomes even more powerful when the people who gave permission pass on content about businesses to their friends. People have always passed on information about businesses to their friends offline, and the social web is now promising to do that online. The social web is making word of mouth *measurable*. We can see who is directly connected to the brand, which of their friends they spoke to, and which of their friends became connected to the brand by consuming their content.

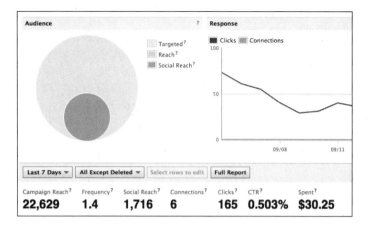

Campaign Reach[7]	Frequency[7]	Social Reach[7]	Connections[7]	Clicks[7]	CTR[7]	Spent[7]
22,629	1.4	1,716	6	165	0.503%	$30.25

We can use tools such as Facebook Insights to see how many friends of friends we have reached (noted as "Social Reach").

We now have a platform capable of delivering permission marketing and word of mouth at a scale that rivals any other communication media. It's possible to gain permission from a relatively small number of people, and reach millions of others through those people's friends. People's social networks scale exponentially. If the average Facebook user has 130 friends,[5] that means that they have approximately 10,000 friends of friends, and over 1,000,000 friends of friends of friends.

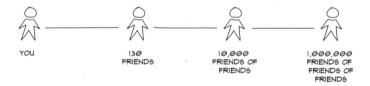

It's hard to see the potential reach of our friends of friends because the network scales beyond our level of comprehension. We are connected to over a million people within three steps.

If a Facebook page has 500,000 fans (fans are people who clicked Like), the friends of those fans total 60 million people. Five million of those people are strong ties. In other words, if these people talk to their closest friends about your business, 5 million people are hearing about your business from someone they trust deeply, and who has a disproportionate amount of influence over them.

In a world of too much information, people turn to their friends

Permission marketing and word of mouth are becoming more important because in a world of too much information, people turn to their friends for advice. Businesses can no longer push information at people and expect it to be absorbed. The world of push marketing is over. Information is more likely to be absorbed if it comes from friends. Aside from the higher level of trust we place in our friends, they will talk about things in a more approachable tone than an official marketing message will.

The social web is making it much easier to get information from our friends about businesses, and people value this. When buying online, 79 percent of people look for the opinions of their strong ties.[6] In fact, because of the breakdown in trust with marketers, they value information from people they don't know over information from the business itself. When 5,000 people were asked what they wanted most from a commercial website, 64 percent ranked "user ratings and reviews" at the top, higher than special offers and price comparison tools, and 49 percent said they wanted more customer testimonials.[7]

Friends are a proxy for relevance

On top of the increasing number of marketing messages we're exposed to, the social web is also generating hundreds of other types of updates, from status updates to photos we're in to emails. This will increase as many updates become passively communicated, for example, the songs we're listening to, the places we visit, the articles we read, the games we play. Passive sharing is the direction that technology is moving. Online, interruption marketing is not only competing with itself, it's competing with activity from friends. And in the vast majority of cases, people care more about hearing from their friends than hearing from a business.

In order for advertising to stand out, it will have to be relevant to people. One way to do this is using people's friends as a signal for relevance. Another way will be better targeting. As people publish more activity online and we learn what they like, we will get really good at only sending messages to people who are interested in our messages. Although people will still only be interested in brands and activities that they already know and prefer, brands they don't know about, or have dismissed, can still be relevant and interesting if people hear about them from a friend.

QUICK TIPS

Draft a new type of marketing plan based on permission, targeting, and people's friends. Use the targeting tools available on Facebook and elsewhere to understand the attributes of different audiences, and the potential reach of people's friends.

Become skilled at building content that people are likely to respond to. Learn by experimenting with different types; what works will be slightly different for every brand. Start by thinking about social behavior offline and how that might work online. Use the information on what people talk about (Chapter 2), and produce content around those patterns.

BUILDING TRUST AND CREDIBILITY

Credibility drives trust, trust drives loyalty

Advertising must build credibility in order to drive sales or influence attitudes. Credibility emerges from a mix of factors such as competence, trustworthiness, expertise, and likability.[8] By far the two most important factors are trustworthiness and expertise. People need to be able to feel that you are truthful, responsible, and won't let them down, and they need to believe that you know what you're talking about. People evaluate trustworthiness and expertise and decide whether a business is credible. Businesses who want to increase loyalty would be much better off focusing on building credibility, and less on measuring frequency of interactions through programs such as frequent flyer miles. Remember that people make most decisions with their emotional brain, and loyalty programs like frequent flyer miles are aimed squarely at our rational brain.

To be trustworthy, businesses will need to be transparent about personal data

The emergence of the social web has led to a lot of information about people that is being stored digitally. We know more and more about what people like, who they know, and who they trust. This information will really help marketers create better marketing programs, and help them ensure that they are only communicating with people who are open to hearing from them. However, before people agree to letting a business know some of their personal information, the business will need to be credible, and the person will need to be able to trust them. People are wary of businesses storing personal information and using it to target advertising,[9] and there is a fine line between people feeling like they are being catered to, and feeling like they are being watched.

The good news is that research has shown that when businesses *are* transparent about what data they have on people, and people have control over that data, they tell advertisers more about themselves.[10] If trustworthiness and expertise are requirements for credibility, then transparency is becoming increasingly critical for building trustworthiness.

Why negative comments are good for your brand

The emergence of the social web means that more people are talking openly about businesses, and many businesses are nervous about any negative commentary. Most want sentiment analysis in the advertising products they use so they can hide the negative comments and only promote the positive comments. But this is the wrong approach. People can easily differentiate between a natural conversation and something that is controlled, and they won't react well to the latter. Hiding negative comments is not transparent; it will dramatically decrease credibility.

If people perceive that a source of information is fair and unbiased, it increases credibility. This is why people trust consumer reports much more than official marketing channels. Sources that sometimes show information that is against their own interests, like negative reviews of their products, are perceived as more credible.

Negative comments about your brand increase your credibility because they strip away the corporate sheen. They make you real. People respond better to things that are real. A brand website, microsite, or Facebook page that shows user generated content that is 100% positive doesn't look real. People have been inundated with push marketing for 20 years. Their default perception is one of skepticism. They can see through the surface layer. People know that no brand is perfect and everyone has room for improvement.

Marketers may be more comfortable with being transparent when they learn that for every negative comment about a brand online, there are eight positive comments.[11] Online, people are overwhelmingly positive about businesses. One reason for this is that in the last 50 years, product quality has dramatically increased. Today, most products meet basic manufacturing quality codes, and they work for a long time.

Friends are a proxy for credibility

We trust our closest friends because we assume that they have our best interests at heart, and that they are honest and tell us the truth. We often buy things solely on a recommendation from a close friend because we trust them. Research has shown that websites recommended to you by a friend are perceived as more credible.[12]

We've seen that friends can be a proxy for relevance. When people see friends recommending or simply being associated with businesses or brands, they are often interested in the connection, despite having little initial interest in the brand. They care about their friends, and so they care about what their friends like, and why. This is critically important for unfamiliar brands and new products. Familiarity leads to trust, and seeing friends connected to businesses builds familiarity.

New forms of advertising such as Sponsored Stories on Facebook are using friends as a proxy for relevance. This is a very different form of advertising than ads that rely on sight, sound, and motion, but can be even more effective. It's based on permission, and on highlighting new things about people's friends.

QUICK TIPS

Building credibility with a business is similar to building trust with someone you just met. It is a slow process, often taking months and even years, and marketers need to be patient. There is no quick solution to creating a credible brand. One way to fast-track it is to be recommended by people's friends.

Don't use sentiment analysis to filter out negative comments, and don't delete negative comments on your Facebook page. Look at it as an opportunity to learn and respond. If people have something negative to say, it's because they had a poor experience with your brand. This is something you should want to rectify rather than hide.

SUMMARY

There are two main problems with interruption marketing, both of which are getting worse. The first is that being interrupted is a terrible experience for people, and it's happening more frequently. The second is that people have a limited amount of time and attention; because more and more marketers are vying for this attention, less and less of them are heard. Because of the exponential increase in the amount of information we're exposed to, increasing reach to gain attention is no longer feasible.

In a world of too much information, people will increasingly turn to their friends. A better approach than interrupting people is to gain their permission to market to them, and use that permission to reach out to their friends. The social web can deliver permission marketing at a scale that rivals any other communication media. Gain permission from a small number of people, and reach millions of their friends.

The emergence of the social web has led to storing a lot of digital information about people. However, to gain this data, businesses will need to be credible and trustworthy. Building credibility requires businesses to be transparent about what data they have, and how they use it.

FURTHER READING

1. For more information on the problems with interruption marketing, see Seth Godin's book *Permission Marketing: Turning Strangers Into Friends And Friends Into Customers* (Simon & Schuster, 1999).

2. See Jay Levinson's book *Guerilla Marketing: Easy and Inexpensive Strategies for Making Big Profits from Your Small Business* (Mariner Books, 2007).

3. See the 1994 research article "The persuasion knowledge model: How people cope with persuasion attempts" by Marian Friestad and Peter Wright.

4. Dan Ariely's experiments are described in his book *Predictably Irrational* (Harper Collins, 2008).

5. See the latest figures at www.facebook.com/press/info.php?statistics.

6. See the 2009 eMarketer report on "Social commerce on Facebook, Twitter and retail sites."

7. Data from a 2008 Forrester research report. See Jeremiah Owyang's post "Who do people trust? (It ain't bloggers)" on his blog Web Strategy.

8. For a deeper discussion on what forms credibility, see Kevin Hogan's book *The Science of Influence* (Wiley, 2010).

9. See the 2009 research paper "Americans reject tailored advertising" by researchers at the University of California, Berkeley, and the University of Pennsylvania.

10. Data from experiments run by bebo.com as reported in Adam Penenberg's book *Viral Loop* (Hyperion, 2010).

11. Multiple research studies confirm this 8:1 ratio. See research by Keller Fay and others at www.bazaarvoice.com/resources/.

12. See research by B.J. Fogg and others at Stanford's Persuasive Technology Lab.

10
Conclusion

THE SOCIAL WEB TODAY

We've covered a lot of ground. Let's first recap the most significant patterns from each chapter, see how they are related, and what it means for the future of your business.

Social networks are not new, and the social web is here to stay

We're social creatures, and social networks have been around for over 10,000 years. The web is being fundamentally rebuilt around people, because our online life is catching up with our offline life. Going forward, the social behavior we've evolved over those thousands of years will be what motivates us to act on the web.

Experiences are better when businesses are built around people, and their friends. This shift will change how we think about marketing, away from "influential" individuals, and towards connected groups of friends.

Sharing is a means to an end

People share information because it makes life easier, builds relationships, and shapes how we appear to others. Eighty percent of our communication is with the 5 to 10 people we are closest to.

We talk about other people, what's around us, and things that generate strong feelings. Most conversations involve recounting personal experiences, or gossiping about who is doing what with whom.

We talk about brands in passing, often driven by what we see in our environment, and to fill a conversation space.

Our social networks are made up of small, independent groups, connected through us

For most of us, our social networks are small. They consist of around five people in our inner circle, 15 people we are very close to, 50 people who we communicate with semi-regularly, 150 people with whom we have stable social relations, and 500 people we loosely know and can recognize.

Most people have four to six independent groups of fewer than 10 friends, and these groups don't overlap. Each one of us uniquely connects multiple groups of people together. This is important because connected groups of friends are required for ideas to spread.

The people closest to us have disproportionate influence over us

We all have unique relationships with everyone in our life and are much closer to some people than to others. Most of us have fewer than 10 strong ties, the people we care about the most, so our circles of trust are very small. The majority of our communication is with our strong ties, and our strong ties hold a disproportionate amount of influence over what we think and do.

We also saw that we communicate infrequently with our weak ties, but that they are often better sources of information than our strong ties are.

When spreading ideas, the structure of the network is more important than the characteristics of individuals

Individuals and hubs are important for ideas to spread. There are two types of hubs. Innovative hubs are a small number of people who are open to new ideas (they have a low threshold), adopt an idea early, and pass it on to a limited number of people. Follower hubs have a larger number of connections and although they often adopt ideas much later than innovative hubs (they have a high threshold), they're more important to reach mass populations.

We saw that when ideas do spread broadly, they are usually started by a regular person, not by someone with special characteristics, commonly referred to as an "influencer." Understanding the network—regular people who are innovative hubs connected to follower hubs as well as people who are easily influenced—is more important than finding special "influential" individuals.

How we behave is learned from observing others

People are heavily influenced by observing the behavior of others around them, and by learning from other people's reactions to their behavior. Culture, and all the social norms associated with that culture, emerges from people observing other people. We are more influenced by the behavior of people in our group, and people we perceive to be like us.

Many of our decisions are made by our nonconscious, emotional brain

Understanding how people influence each other requires us to study the relationships between things. One important relationship is the one between our conscious, rational brain and our nonconscious, emotional brain. Most consumer behavior models are built on the idea that people are rational thinkers. But we make a minority of decisions with our rational brain. Most of our behavior and decision-making is driven by our emotional brain, which we can't access.

Our brain doesn't remember details because it needs to prioritize what it stores in memory. It remembers relationships, and makes up details to fill in the gaps in memory.

We're wired to avoid trying new things, especially when they don't match our beliefs

Our pre-existing beliefs dramatically influence how we respond to new things. We try to act consistently with our past behavior, and when presented with information that conflicts with our existing beliefs, our natural reaction is to deny the new information.

Changing people's attitudes is incredibly hard, but changing their behavior is easier. Starting with small requests for behavioral change often eventually leads to attitudinal change.

People will increasingly turn to their friends for information

The amount of information accessible to us is increasing exponentially, but our capacity for processing ideas and memory will remain the same. In a world of too much information, marketing and advertising based on interrupting people, or trying to shift their attention from something else, is a race to the bottom.

In this information rich world that we have created, people will increasingly turn to their friends for advice. Marketing will need to focus activities on gaining permission to market to people by being credible, trustworthy, interesting, and useful, and by marketing to small, connected groups of friends.

THE NEXT FEW YEARS

Rebuilding your business around people is not a choice

Facebook, Twitter, and Zynga are overwhelming evidence of the shift to a web built around people. The social web is not a temporary trend. Make no mistake—this is a permanent change. Over the next five years, this shift will dramatically change entire business sectors. New companies that we have not yet heard of, built around people, will grow to multibillion dollar businesses. Zynga was the first. Music service Spotify or DIY marketplace Etsy might be the next. If your business doesn't adapt, and restructure itself around people, a competitor will, and they will most likely render you obsolete. The only certain thing about the social web is that one of your competitors will embrace it, and build things you can't compete with—unless you embraced it also.

A new knowledge set is required

Anyone involved in building and selling products—designers, marketers, developers, advertisers—will need to understand three related things:

1. Social behavior. Understanding people's behavior has always been important to good design and marketing, but has never been considered a prerequisite for success. However, now that the web is being rebuilt with people at the center, studying people's social behavior will become critical. You now have an understanding of why people do what they do, why they share some information but not everything, what they talk about and don't talk about, and how they observe the behavior of others to understand how to act. Use the references cited to further your understanding of social behavior.

2. Networks. It is hard to visualize our own social network, never mind multiple social networks joined together. Yet understanding how networks work will become a requirement for success on the web. You now have an understanding of how networks scale, from our friends, through friends of friends, and through their friends. Use the references cited to further your understanding of networks.

3. How people think. Lots of our decisions and behavior are influenced by both what is stored in our nonconscious brain (our biases), and by the calculations that our nonconscious brain makes. You now have an understanding of the relationships and interactions between people, between people and products, and how people perceive the world. Use the references cited to further your understanding of how people think.

This book is the first important step in acquiring this new knowledge set. The next step is to take what you have learned and try many small experiments. Experimenting and failing is how the best technology companies innovate. Evolve by measuring what works and discarding things that don't work.

Focus on many small, independent groups of friends

People are most heavily influenced by the people they are emotionally closest to. These are also the people who they communicate with the most, socialize with the most, and trust the most. Marketing needs to focus on strong ties, and on the many small, independent yet connected groups of friends.

Remember that it is incredibly hard to find people with large degrees of influence over many others—if they exist at all. All of us are influential on some topics, and all of us have a little influence on other topics. All of us can spread messages because we all connect multiple independent groups of friends together.

Focus your energy on understanding why people share, and on using that understanding to create products and content that will be shared by small groups of close friends. If you manage this, people will naturally share your content with their friends, and those friends will naturally share with their own friends. Your message will reach millions of people, passed on by their most trusted sources.

ACKNOWLEDGMENTS

Thanks to the different groups in my life who helped me get this book out the door.

Work group

Thanks to

- All the people who conducted the research that was cited in *Grouped*. Without your great work this book wouldn't exist.
- The many people working on the social web, with whom I've had the pleasure of endlessly debating the social behavior we're observing, the implications of it, and how we might design and build things that people will love and value.
- Authors and bloggers whose invaluable content on related topics has consistently been a great source of knowledge and inspiration to me. To the people who provide commentary on blogs—your commentary is often the most insightful part of the conversation.
- Joshua Porter, for encouraging me to get my stuff out there, and helping me find my voice.
- Conference organizers who have allowed me to speak at their events and given me a platform to share my ideas.

Family group

Thanks to

- My wife Jenny, who put up with a missing husband for many evenings and weekends for months on end.
- My family. Without the love and support of my parents Gerard and Niamh, my brothers Conor and Neil, and my sisters Aoife and Irene, I'd never be in the position I find myself in.
- Toby, who sat within two feet of me for almost all my writing.

Dublin group, London group, San Francisco group

Thanks to

· All my different friend groups for letting me go on about this book when there were more interesting things to talk about. To my Dublin friends, to my London friends, to my San Francisco friends. You know who you are.

· Fiona and Darina, my original cheerleaders.

Book group

Thanks to

· All the fantastic folks at Peachpit who made this book a reality. In particular, thanks to Michael Nolan, Rose Weisburd, Mimi Heft, and Nancy Ruenzel. Michael, for initially encouraging me to write about my work and providing encouragement and support ever since. Rose, my development editor, who made this book far better than I could ever have hoped for. Mimi, for designing a great cover and layout, and putting up with my many requests. Nancy, for consistently supporting the project.

· All the people who reviewed parts of the book and gave me feedback on the content.

· The readers of my blog, thinkoutsidein.com, whose commentary always gives me new perspectives and helps me shape many early thoughts.

New groups

Thanks to you, for reading. I hope we'll chat together face to face in a future group.

INDEX

A

adoption thresholds   74–75, 76, 81
advertising
    historical increase in   132
    new forms of   135, 142
    reach approach to   133
    targeted   80, 138, 139
    See also marketing
Airbnb service   46
Allen, Christopher   48
American Eagle Outfitters   41
American Express   120
anchoring   126
Apple products   122
Ariely, Dan   98, 128, 131, 144
associates   52

B

Bahrami, Bahador   92
Barabási, Albert-László   31, 48
basic friendship pattern   55
behavior
    changing   123–124, 149
    consistency of   118–119
    consumer   12, 104, 106, 148
    influence of   86–87, 109, 148
    social proof and   86–87
    technology and   9–10
    understanding   150
beliefs   120, 149
Berger, Jonah   19, 27, 28
Bernoff, Josh   28, 69, 99
biases
    confirmation bias   127
    environmental cues and
        125–126
    habits related to   123–124
    influenced by others   118–119
    perception of value and
        120–122
BMW ads   19, 26

Bok, Derek   27
boyd, danah   32, 48
brain
    conscious   103, 107–109
    decision making and
        103–104, 107, 109–110, 148
    memory and   111–113
    nonconscious   103–104,
        107–111, 148
    patterns detected by   105, 110
brands, conversations about   20–21
broad friendship pattern   58
Broadbent, Stefana   14, 68
Brooks, David   48

C

Call of Duty games   2, 3
cascades of ideas   73, 80, 81
choices, number of   120–121, 122
Christakis, Nicholas   48, 68, 94, 97
Cialdini, Robert   98
classic sales funnel   104, 106, 113
Cohen, Jonathan   128
comforters   53
communal laughter   16
comparison   126
confidants   53
confirmation bias   127
Connected (Christakis and Fowler)
    48, 68, 97
connections
    degrees of separation between
        43–45
    independent groups and
        network   39
    influence not correlated
        with   73
    marketing campaigns for
        making   18
    social network patterns of
        33–35, 47
    surfacing of common   45
conscious brain   103, 107–109
    decision making by   103, 110
    processing capacity of
        107, 108

WATCH READ CREATE

Unlimited online access to all Peachpit, Adobe Press, Apple Training and New Riders videos and books, as well as content from other leading publishers including: O'Reilly Media, Focal Press, Sams, Que, Total Training, John Wiley & Sons, Course Technology PTR, Class on Demand, VTC and more.

No time commitment or contract required! Sign up for one month or a year.
All for $19.99 a month

SIGN UP TODAY
peachpit.com/creativeedge

creative edge